THE
QABALAH
WORKBOOK FOR
MAGICIANS

A GUIDE TO THE SEPHIROTH

ANITA KRAFT

WEISERBOOKS
San Francisco, CA / Newburyport, MA

First published in 2013 by Weiser Books
Red Wheel/Weiser, LLC
With offices at:
665 Third Street, Suite 400
San Francisco, CA 94107
www.redwheelweiser.com

Library of Congress Cataloging-in-Publication Data

Kraft, Anita.
    The Qabalah workbook for magicians : a guide to the Sephiroth / Anita Kraft.
      pages cm
    Includes bibliographical references.
    ISBN 978-1-57863-535-1
    1. Cabala. I. Title.
BF1623.C2K73 2013
135'.47--dc23   2013006172

Cover design by Jim Warner
Cover image by Athanasius Kircher
Interior by Kathryn Sky-Peck
Typeset in Adobe Garamond

A note from the author regarding the cover image:
Athanasius Kircher lived in the seventeenth century. He was a Jesuit and is considered the founder
of Egyptology. Kircher created this version of the Tree of Life, perhaps the most recognized tree in
occultism. His version of the Tree contains what many today consider mistakes. I maintain that there
are no mistakes in Qabalah, only different perspectives on the universe. Nevertheless, there have
been many changes in the correspondences to the Tree, mostly owing to the Golden Dawn. I use this
image as a nod to Kircher and his contributions to Hermetic Qabalah.

Printed in the United States of America
TS

10 9 8 7 6 5 4 3 2 1
The paper used in this publication meets the minimum requirements of the American National
Standard for Information Sciences—Permanence of Paper for Printed Library Materials
Z39.48-1992 (R1997).

DEDICATION

Over twenty years ago, I was looking for answers. I walked into an occult bookstore and the man working there decided I was a bored housewife and sent me away with a—how shall I say?—lightweight book. I read it and it was not my cup of tea. I went back and asked the same man if he had something a little more academic and substantial. He then gave me Magick in Theory and Practice *by Aleister Crowley. He took me to a Gnostic Mass and I found what I had been looking for all those years.*

We have been through much together—a love affair, a breakup, and now we have a lifelong friendship. He is my mentor, my teacher, my student, and, most important, he is my friend. Our journey these twenty-plus years has been amazing.

Randall introduced me to my path, and stood by me while the path worked on me. It was very difficult in the beginning, unlearning a lifetime of bad habits, thoughts, and beliefs. But he stood by me even when most would not. From Randall, I learned so much; but above all, I learned patience, kindness, and fraternity. I don't know anyone who keeps his fraternal oaths and bonds more purely than Randall.

Randall encouraged me to write this book. He knew I reached a whole different audience with my teaching methods and approach to Qabalah. I have finally realized this project with his help and guidance and, most important, his editing and proofreading.

I dedicate this work to my friend, my soulmate, and my Woobie. Thank you Randall, Frater Leo, for all your love.

CONTENTS

Acknowledgments vii

Foreword *by Lon Milo DuQuette*. 1

Introduction 9

How to Use This Workbook. 15

How Not to Lose Your Mind *by Keith Taylor* 29

The Sephiroth 35

The Supernal Triad. 43

    Kether 48

    Chokmah 57

    Binah. 65

    Reviewing the Supernal Triad:

        The Union of Chokmah and Binah 72

The Second Triad 77

    Chesed. 80

    Gevurah. 87

    Tiphareth. 98

    Reviewing the Second Triad. 106

The Third Triad 109

    Netzach 112

    Hod. 120

    Yesod 128

    Reviewing the Third Triad 135

Malkuth, the Gateway 139
    Malkuth. 140

Conclusion. 149
Appendix A: Additional Exercises. 151
Appendix B: Crowley's *777* Chart 157
References 162

ACKNOWLEDGMENTS

I have many people to thank for helping me over the years. First, thank you to Keith Taylor, who listened, typed, listened, retyped this work. Also for working the workbook while I put the book together and providing direct feedback on the material. Your assistance was invaluable.

Also thank you to the following people who have been teachers and magical mentors over the years: Dan German, Elke Goodman Bussen, Dionysius Rogers, and Randall Bowyer. Thank you to Angela Landrith for inspiring me to put my classes on paper.

Thanks to my kids, April and Anthony. Thanks to my mother, Gloria, who always encouraged me, even when she didn't understand what I was doing. Thanks to the members of the various camps and oases, brothers and sisters with whom I have interacted, whom I have taught, and who have taught me about magick and fraternity.

Thank you to the OTO and our leaders for their service and assistance, both directly and indirectly—Hymenaeus Beta, Sabazius X°, and Rodney Orpheus.

Especially thank you to my bishop and my friend, Lon Milo DuQuette, who believed in me and supported me, and who has encouraged me over the years. Your support and words of wisdom have changed my life and most definitely assisted me in this work.

Foreword by
Lon Milo DuQuette

The Qabalah is not a belief system. It's a way of looking at things. It's a way of organizing your universe so neatly that you eventually discover your own place in it.

Rabbi Lamed Ben Clifford[1]

I am an old hippie. In 1967, however, I was a *young* hippie. I had very long hair, dressed in colorful sweatshirts and karate pants. I went barefoot a lot. More important, I had enthusiastically embarked (with the aid of psychoactive chemicals and the works of Paramahansa Yogananda, Alan Watts, Dr. Timothy Leary, and the Beatles) upon a journey of self-exploration and discovery that continues to this day.

The mid-1960s were a cosmic aberration—a crack in space-time. It was certainly a remarkable season of history; an exhilarating and magical age to be alive and young. In that golden moment, it was possible for a shallow young bumpkin from Nebraska—possessed of no more intelligence or wisdom than a turnip—to stumble naïvely into the *sanctum sanctorum* of Montsalvat and, with cud-chewing nonchalance, take a good long slurp from the Holy Grail. I came away from those early psychedelic experiences with the Technicolor realization that God is consciousness— consciousness is the secret of existence; consciousness is the secret of life— and that *I am consciousness.*

---

1   Lon Milo DuQuette, *The Chicken Qabalah of Rabbi Lamed Ben Clifford* (York Beach, ME: Weiser Books. 2001), p. 150.

Mind-expanding drugs were just what was needed to blast open the heavily barricaded doors of my constipated and medieval perception; but once that gate was duly and truly breached, I was faced with the fact that the obstacles that remained in my path would be far more subtle and difficult to remove. These occlusions would require the use of more delicate ordnance. For spiritual nutrients, I grazed upon the obligatory classics of Buddhist and Hindu literature, and I graduated from drugs to the quiet disciplines of meditation and Eastern mysticism. I cut my hair, went vegetarian, and fancied myself a yogi.

Yes! I was all prepared to be a first-class Eastern mystic—at least, I thought that's where I was going. Something, however, just didn't seem right. On an intellectual level, I had no difficulty grasping the mystical concept that I (my *real* self) was something profoundly more than my body and my thoughts and my emotions. I understood that my *real self* was, in essence, the perfect reflection of the absolute and Supreme Consciousness (that great "whatever-it-is" within that resides in everything, and of which the manifested universe is just an expression). It was perfectly clear to me that if I could only strip away all the things that I was *not,* then the only thing remaining would be exactly that—*The Only Thing*—and that Only Thing would be both the Supreme Consciousness *and* me!

This, I concluded with youthful certainty, was what Eastern mystics were shooting for. This level of consciousness is the profound "nothingness" of Nirvana—the wall-to-wall totality of Samadhi. All I had to do was "strip down" to my most naked me—and when I got there, my "I-ness" would disappear into the big "whatever-it-is-ness" of the Supreme Consciousness.

But alas, I was a very poor meditator. Oh, I could look like a pretty good meditator. I could sit still in my asana for long periods of time with a full teacup and saucer balanced on my head.[2] My skill in pranayama was admirable, and I could hold the clear image of a working pendulum clock in my mind's eye for eternal micro-seconds at a time. But something was profoundly wrong with my work; and I'll wager that the astute reader has probably already identified exactly what was wrong with my view of this

---

2 Really! Ask Constance. She had to put that full teacup on my head each morning!

whole enlightenment business. Here—I'll say it for you: "Mr. DuQuette, for a mystic, you use the word 'I' an awful lot. Aren't you supposed to lose your ego as you near enlightenment?"

Bingo! Guilty as charged! I knew, of course, that eventually we must transcend identity with the ego to become the absolute Supreme Consciousness (just as we must transcend our identity with the body and the emotions and the mind). But for the life of me, I couldn't remove the objective "me" in the subjective "dissolution-of-me" process. I couldn't shake the idea of how *cool* I was going to look gaining enlightenment—how cool I was going to look with *no ego!*

At first, I felt a little embarrassed about all this. But, as serious self-condemnation has never been one of my virtues, I soon came to the giddy realization that I was simply trying to play Eastern software on my Western hardware. Perhaps I was hardwired by nature and Western civilization not to seek divine union by *stripping away* all the things I *am not*, but instead by *uniting* myself with all the things that *I am.* Profound *emptiness* and profound *fullness* are one and the same. The disciplines of the East oblige the mystic to look inward for union with God; and that's great for the Eastern, introspective disposition. The Western psyche, on the other hand, is inclined to look outward. We love scripture and ritual drama that gives outward expression to inward realities. In either case, the supreme goal is the same. Which approach one takes is simply a matter of one's cultural temperament. I'm as Western as they come. So I'm an "out-y."

I turned my attention to what the West might have to offer, and began my search for "Western software"—a Western equivalent to the Tao, a Western equivalent to Zen—and I more or less found what I was looking for in the Qabalah.

My introduction to the Qabalah was the indirect result of my youthful involvement with the Rosicrucian Order AMORC.[3] Encouraged by my older brother, Marc, I had joined the Order in the early 1970s in hopes it would give me something spiritual and wholesome to occupy my nervous

---

3 AMORC. Ancient and Mystical Order Rosae Crucis, an international fraternal organization founded in 1915 by advertising executive Harvey Spencer Lewis and others.

energy as I transitioned from the recording artist's life of sex, drugs, and rock 'n' roll to the docility of a domesticated husband and father.

AMORC's monograph teachings were delivered promptly each week by mail. They were an offbeat combination of solitary ritual meditations and junior high science and chemistry experiments. Much as I had hated school, I found the AMORC material oddly fascinating and inspiring. I was nothing short of ecstatic when I attended my first "convocation" service at a local lodge in Long Beach. I discovered then and there that I absolutely loved dressing up in spooky robes, intoning strange chants, and strutting around in the dark.

As I ascended up the degree structure of the organization, I learned that certain mystical perks could be redeemed. I was informed by a fellow member that, when I reached a certain degree level, I would qualify to order and receive additional monograph instructions in certain mystically related subjects. One such extracurricular monograph series was on "The Holy Kabbalah," and I impatiently awaited the time when I would be qualified to register for the teachings. When that day finally arrived, I sent off a money order for the course and eagerly awaited my initiation into the mysteries of the Holy Kabbalah.

The six monographs arrived in one envelope and I read all six in one sitting. They contained a brief historical sketch and a bibliography, but no meditations, no rituals or exercises. Indeed, there was nothing that made any sense to me at all. In fact, most of the text was filled with dire warnings to the student about what the Kabbalah is *not*. I cannot resist satirically paraphrasing:

- Kabbalah is spelled "Kabbalah." If you run across literature that spells it with only one "B," it is not really Kabbalah and you should run away from it. If you run across literature that spells it with a "Q" or a "C," or indeed in any way other than "Kabbalah," it is not real Kabbalah and you should stop reading and run away.

- Kabbalah is not something that is written down, so don't expect to discover anything about it by reading stuff. Kabbalah is only passed orally from one pious Jewish man (over the age of forty but under eighty, who is rich enough to have a lot of leisure time to devote to studying Kabbalah) to another Jewish man (over the age of forty but under eighty, who is also rich enough to have a lot of leisure time to devote to studying Kabbalah).

- Kabbalah has nothing to do with a diagram called the Tree of Life—if you see a Tree of Life, run away!

- Kabbalah has nothing to do with the Tarot cards—if you see Tarot cards, run away!

- Kabbalah has nothing to do with magic—if you see anything to do with magic, run away!

- Kabbalah is the secret, esoteric, hidden, forbidden, furtive, and most likely *dangerous* study of the Holy Bible and it is certainly not for presumptuous young dilettantes like *you*. In fact, you should be embarrassed for even being curious as to what Kabbalah might be about. Thank you for waiting two years for these monographs and for sending $15.00. Now— *run away!*[4]

That was in 1972. Things have changed in the world of Qabalah! Kabbalah, Cabala, Qabalah is everywhere; books, lessons, teachings, organizations, even videos, movies, and CDs can be purchased, attended, viewed, and listened to whenever you like. What remains a rarity, however, are competent, practical instructions as to how actually to incorporate the fundamentals of Qabalah into one's daily life and routine. For me, it has been a hit-and-miss comedy of errors and accidental triumphs, and perhaps that's how it should always be. But it is clear to me that the work needn't be harder on the poor student than absolutely necessary.

---

4 Of course I'm exaggerating. I have the greatest respect for the organization, and except for this outrageously discouraging set of monographs have nothing but wonderful memories of my AMORC experiences.

How can today's serious student actually begin the process of inoculating himself or herself with the virus of Qabalastic thought—that divine disease that eventually incubates in the soul and hatches as illumination? How does a modern mystic go about connecting everything in the universe with everything else until there is no "anything else" left?

In an attempt to answer those questions, I wrote a little book that I whimsically called *The Chicken Qabalah of Rabbi Lamed Ben Clifford.*[5] It was, quite frankly, the text I wish I could have read when I first began my Qabalah adventure. Over the years, the book has been well received and, for the most part, I am satisfied that my labor has been rewarded. I am especially gratified that it was chosen by Ms. Anita Kraft as one of the source books for her marvelous *Qabalah Workbook for Magicians.* Her work is that rarest of magical tools—an elegant, hands-on course in practical Qabalah. It is a book that obliges you to roll up your sleeves and do things with the Qabalah. I am particularly thrilled because reading her book has afforded me the opportunity to witness a new generation of Qabalistic magicians whose brilliance shines, not only from the fact that she "gets it" in the traditional sense, but also because she is pushing the technology forward in fresh, innovative, and exhilarating ways. I am proud to be in a small measure associated with its publication.

In closing, I would like to leave you with the last seventy-two words uttered by my favorite Qabalah teacher and (until his mysterious disappearance a few years ago) our family's life-long spiritual counselor, Rabbi Lamed Ben Clifford. The dear man once told me: "Ron"—he never could remember my name—"Ron, the Qabalah is not a belief system. It's a way of looking at things. It's a way of organizing your universe so neatly that you eventually discover your own place in it."

It is my sincerest wish that this little book will aid and comfort you as you organize *your* universe so neatly that you will eventually discover your own place in it.

Bless you all. *Shalom.*

---

5 DuQuette, *The Chicken Qabalah.*

THE SECRET OF
THE SHEM-HA MEPHORASH

THE LAST WRITTEN WORDS OF
RABBI LAMED BEN CLIFFORD[6]

God is.
Undivided God is pure potentiality and realizes Nothing.

God can only realize Itself by becoming Many and then experiencing all pos-
sibilities through the adventures of Its many parts.

The ultimate purpose for My existence is to exhaust
My individual potentiality.

My Love of God and God's love of Me springs from
the Great Secret we share.

The Secret is

God and I will achieve Supreme Enlightenment at the same moment.

LON MILO DUQUETTE

---

6 DuQuette, *The Chicken Qabalah,* p. 202.

Introduction

was raised in the Catholic ghetto. I spent most of my childhood in Catholic schools and organizations and playing with Catholic friends. My entire world revolved around the Catholic Church.

When I was in my early twenties, on a silent retreat, I had an intense vision. It left me ecstatic and overwhelmed. Like most people, I interpreted the experience in the cultural context I had at the time—I believed I had been visited by Jesus. I believed I had a vocation and pursued becoming a nun.

A very wise nun at the convent told me she thought I needed to search some more. Honestly, I don't think they knew what to do with someone who had undergone a real mystical experience. However, I knew that being a Bride of Christ was my destiny. I left the convent and the Church and set about to make sense of this vision. Nine years later, I attended my first Gnostic Mass at Porta Lucis Oasis of the Ordo Templi Orientis in Indianapolis, and I knew I was about to find the answers I had been seeking.

I earnestly set about learning magick and became instantly attracted to Qabalah. I understood the concept of the Sabbath Bride and my first magical motto was *Soror Shekinah*. I understood being a Bride of Christ from an entirely different perspective. I knew I had found my path and the organization that would nourish and foster my growth and development toward my true will.

Thus began a twenty-year journey into the mystical and magical universe that is Qabalah.

When I first began to study Qabalah, I started with the usual material available. People told me to read *Kabbalah Unveiled* by Mathers, or *Mystical Qabalah* by Fortune. I continued to read and to try to understand what I was reading. I read *Gates of Light* by Gikatilla and *Sefer Yetzirah* by Kaplan. In fact, I read anything I could find.

Finally, I took an excellent class at Indiana University on Jewish mysticism, in which I explored the distinction between theoretical Qabalah and practical Qabalah. I had been studying the theory; now it was time for the practice. Unfortunately for me, there really weren't a lot of books on how to be a practical Qabalist.

I started my own workings. I am a sensual person. I need my work to be tactile, interactive; I need it to be physical. So I started working with altars. My understanding of theoretical Qabalah grew as my practical work continued. It really wasn't long before everything in my universe was in my Qabalistic universe. They became one and the same.

Over the years, as I interacted with others, I heard people say: "I don't like Qabalah; it's too complicated." Or my favorite: "I am not academic and it's too hard." I took this on as a challenge. I have fifteen years of experience as a corporate trainer and I know that I can teach anyone anything. It's not the material; it's the media used.

Magick depends heavily on written texts to transfer information and to teach. Unfortunately, for most of us, this method of instruction is not the best way to learn. Most people learn primarily from doing something; reading books and hearing lectures are secondary modes of learning. So if the only material available is reading-based and not practice-based, we leave out a huge portion of the population who could be great Qabalists.

With my training skills, I was able to translate the written material into active "doing" material for myself. I decided to try to do this for others. I started teaching classes on how to *do*, not just how to read, Qabalah. I used all three learning methods—reading, listening, and doing—to reach the maximum audience. Each time I taught the class, I was encouraged to write a book based on my material. It always made me chuckle to think of writing a book to teach students how to *do* Qabalah that went beyond the books. The point of the class was to reach more people than writing did.

Finally, I decided to do something. The publication of *The Chicken Qabalah of Rabbi Lamed Ben Clifford* by Lon Milo DuQuette went a long way toward making Qabalah accessible to more people. I decided I would write a workbook that gave tactile and practical exercises to accompany the written material, focusing on *Chicken Qabalah* with a few other primary texts. This workbook is the culmination of that decision.

I took reading material and provided exercises to help solidify the information. I know many people who have studied Qabalah will think this is not for them, or that they already "get it." *Doing*, not just reading—getting outside of Hod—and experiencing Qabalah with this workbook will greatly enhance your understanding of the material. You will take your understanding of Qabalah to a new level.

Qabalah is experiential, as are mysticism and magick. If all you do is read, you are not a mystic, magician, or Qabalist. You must do!

During the rise of Qabalah in the twelfth and thirteenth centuries, there were Jewish mystical groups called *circles*. These were study groups composed of teachers and students whose goal was to preserve the purity (or elitism) of the Jewish mystical practice. These circles developed an elaborate system of symbols and metaphors. Their material, however, is narrative-based and reading Qabalistic theory can be confusing. It's a bit of a circle in itself, in that understanding the narrative requires insight into Qabalistic symbolism, yet it's the narrative that gives us the symbols.

The material of these circles was published, but only in theoretical and symbolical stories such as the Zohar, which became a canonical Jewish text. "How-to" Qabalah was considered secret and dangerous. Rules were put into place restricting the study of Qabalah. One required that at least two people be present when studying Qabalah; another required that students be men over forty years old. There are elaborate tales of the dangers of Qabalah and the mystical journey, including blindness and death. Qabalah involves visions and interpretations of those visions, and the Rabbis would not have wanted just anyone developing their own views of God or of the Torah. So they made their mystical practices scary and inaccessible.

Christians—and Christian magicians—translated and absorbed Qabalah into their practices. Christians adopted Qabalah because they believed it confirmed the Trinity. In fact, the first publications of the Zohar were done by two Christian Italian publishing houses.

Eventually, because of the Jewish Enlightenment, Qabalah was viewed as superstitious nonsense. This occurred at the same time as the rise in mysticism and magical practice in Western Esotericism in Europe in the 1800s. Qabalah grew beyond its original foundations in Gnosticism, Neo-Platonism, and Jewish mysticism, to become the primary method of mystical and magical attainment in the Western Esoteric movement.

Qabalah means "tradition" and the tradition that is Qabalah is change. Every Qabalist has made changes and helped with the evolution of the understanding of God and subsequently of the universe. At times, men have come along and discouraged changes in Qabalah—unfortunately so, in my view. I have always felt that it is part of being a Qabalistic teacher to encourage students to make Qabalah their own.

So much goes into understanding existence—culture, history, perceptions, language, just overall experiences—that it is improbable that any two people will use the exact same symbols to represent their universe. All Qabalists must make changes. Qabalah is your universe, and my universe is not the same as yours.

With that said, however, there can be common ground. Here is an example. Five people go to New York City. All five are asked to describe the experience. No two people, even if they attended the exact same events, will describe their experiences identically. Their experiences will be understood in the context of their perspectives and what is important or relevant to them, even though they all went to the same city.

Qabalah is similar. The Sephiroth are what they are. They are specific and defined. Yet my experience, vision, view, and encounters with each will be different from anyone else's. This difference is what makes up the tradition of Qabalah. It is what makes the universe of the Qabalah alive and vibrant. It is both a personal and a common shared experience. It's magick.

Qabalah can be as simple or as complex as you want to make it. It can be as simple as the Sephiroth and the Paths. The *Sefer Yetzirah*, the text from which we get the Sephiroth and Paths, is a short work. It doesn't contain Gematria, Notariqon, or elaborate correspondences. It is the creation of the universe using the Hebrew alphabet and ten Sephiroth. In my opinion, this is all one needs to learn in order to become a practicing Qabalistic magician.

Qabalah contains four worlds, each associated with one of the four elements—Fire, Water, Air, Earth. Each world builds upon the previous world. Exploring the four worlds in greater detail is the topic for an entire book in itself, but a basic understanding of this concept is necessary for this workbook. The four worlds are Atziluth (The World of Emanation, associated with Fire), Briah (The World of Creation, associated with Water), Yetzirah (The World of Formation, associated with Air), and Assiah (The World of Physical Manifestation, associated with Earth).

This workbook starts with the world of Assiah (Earth) and the world of Yetzirah (Air). The world of Assiah is the material world. It's the world where all things physical exist. It is also the location of our animalistic needs and tendencies—the world of eating, sleeping, and base animal functions.

The world of Yetzirah is Air. It's the world where our instincts are transformed into action, where we begin to transcend the instinctual world and move to the intellectual and formative world. For example, I kill an animal because I am hungry. Yetzirah says that if I make a fire and cook it, it will taste better. If I add certain herbs, it will taste great.

It's important to ground our understanding of Qabalah in these two worlds so that we can ascend into the worlds of intuition and spiritual attainment—Briah and Atziluth. The exercises in this book are designed to develop the physical and intellectual foundation of each Sephirah.[1]

In Appendix A, you will find additional exercises that you can do once you have developed a solid foundation and basic understanding of the Sephiroth. Crowley said that the feeling of banishing is unmistakable. So too is it for magick and mysticism. You will know when you have moved into the Qabalistic universe. Your universe will merge with the Qabalah and you will see no difference between the two.

—ANITA KRAFT

---

[1] For additional explanations on the Four Worlds, you can read Lon Milo DuQuette, *The Chicken Qabalah* (York Beach, ME: Weiser Books, 2001), chapter 6, part I, "The Four Qabalistic Worlds."

How to Use This Workbook

his workbook complements Qabalistic and magical works already available. The exercises presented here will aid in your understanding of the Tree of Life and other Qabalistic concepts.

I have given basic information that will allow you to begin to understand the Sephiroth. However, I will also make recommendations and point you to additional resources where the information is further explained. Reading the extra information is not required to do the workbook exercises. But when you finish, you may want to follow up with some of these works. They will enhance your understanding.

The primary reading materials I used when creating this workbook are:

- *Thoth Tarot Deck* by Aleister Crowley. There are a few variations published by US Games or you can use any deck you prefer. I use Crowley's *Thoth Deck* and this workbook references it throughout.

- *The Chicken Qabalah of Rabbi Lamed Ben Clifford* by Lon Milo DuQuette

- *Understanding Aleister Crowley's Thoth Tarot* by Lon Milo DuQuette

- *Magick: Liber ABA, Book Four* by Aleister Crowley

- *777 and Other Qabalistic Writings* by Aleister Crowley

ADDITIONAL TEXTS

There are also additional suggested readings that will enhance your understanding of the exercises.

- Bhagavad Gita

- *Liber Cheth vel Vallum Abiegni sub figurâ CLVI*, Appendix of *Magick: Liber ABA, Book Four* by Aleister Crowley

- *Liber Librae sub figurâ XXX*, Appendix of *Magick: Liber ABA, Book Four* by Aleister Crowley or *Equinox* Vol III Number 10

- *The Hymn of the Robe of Glory* by G. R. S. Mead (available online)

- *Liber Aleph vel CXI* by Aleister Crowley

- *Sefer Yetzirah* by Aryeh Kaplan

Don't underestimate the limitless amount of information on the Internet as well. Research plants, stones, perfumes, etc. and study their information. Remember to record in your journal everything that pertains to the Sephiroth. Expand your understanding by researching items as you study, synthesize, and solidify your understanding of the material.

A bibliography of all the books and articles I have read and written over the years is included at the end of this book, along with a suggested reading list. If you are interested, they make excellent reading.

JOURNALING

You will need a journal to record all of your experiences and experiments from the exercises in this workbook. It is recommended that you obtain a sketchbook type of journal so that you can draw as well as write. I draw in my journal as much as I write.

ALTAR ITEMS

Parts of the exercises in the workbook ask you to acquire and furnish various altars for each of the Sephiroth. For these altars, you will need to obtain certain items that will be used during the exercises. You can create these items yourself or purchase them. At your discretion, you may also make logical substitutions.

Do not feel as if you need to use or understand *all* of the attributions or items on your first trip through the Sephiroth. You can choose to go through them learning only their colors, names, and meanings. You can work through the book as many times as you want, adding to your knowledge with each pass. Perhaps the first time through, you may skip the Tarot associations, then come back through again and add those at a later time.

Work at your own level and ability to synthesize the information. I give you a lot of details. Choose what you will to work, and understand that you can work this book as many times as you want.

SUPPLEMENTAL WEBSITE MATERIAL

www.magickqabalah.com

This website is available to all students of this workbook. Here you will find additional downloadable worksheets, supplemental exercises, items for your altars, a forum to share your insights with others, and a means to communicate with the authors. You can ask us questions, seek clarification, and give feedback on your experiences.

ALTARS

The first exercise for each Sephirotic working is to acquire an altar and the necessary items for it. Your altar is where you will begin all of your Sephirotic exercises. It is your gateway to the Sephiroth and should be constructed appropriately. Much of the learning process for this workbook comes from researching and acquiring items for your altar.

In placing items on your altars, focus on building anchors that will help you both understand and experience the Sephiroth on a personal level. I have supplied examples of things that you should have and use for your altars. However, if you have additional items that you associate with the Sephiroth that you feel will benefit your understanding of them, by all means, use them. Be sure to document in your journal why you make the associations.

Your altars can be constructed or purchased. They should accommodate all of the items you'll be placing on them. You may use a cube, a TV tray, or a little round three-legged table available at a big-box retailer. Your altars don't have to be expensive and you will need multiple altars as we go along. They should all be the same size.

Each chapter devoted to a Sephirah details the required, recommended, and optional items to place on your altar. For more information regarding any of these items, refer to the appropriate sections in the *777* tables in Appendix B.

ALTAR CLOTHS

You can use any of the color scales in *777*. I always use the Queen Scale colors; they are the easiest with which to identify, since they are the most commonly used. For each Sephirah, create or purchase an altar cloth to cover your altar. It needs to be large enough to cover your altar completely. I have used felt squares and large handkerchiefs, and have even made some very elaborate altar cloths. Don't underestimate the important magical weapon—*the Labor of Preparation!*

ZODIACAL REPRESENTATION

Each Sephirah on the Tree of Life represents an astrological body (i.e., a planet, a constellation, etc.). On your altar, place a representation of that astrological body. You may need to be creative here, but there are lots of options available to you—3-D science spheres, hand-painted Styrofoam balls, or emblems on the altar cloth itself. (My friend and brother, Keith, has iron-on patches of the planets and their astrological symbols that he attaches to his altar cloths. I made circles using the color of the Sephirah and put the symbols on the circle. See figure 2 on page 38.) These should also have the astrological symbol on them. Example: Saturn is ♄, Venus is ♀.

As with many of the items you can place on your altar, pictures or photos of the planets may be used; however, these should be used only as a last resort. The object here is to create an experience for all of your senses, including touch. It is better to create, paint, sculpt, or cut out an imperfect creation of your own than to use a picture someone else made. You will, throughout your practices, pick up and hold the objects on your altar regularly. Pictures are excellent visual representations, but they lack this tactile dimension.

You can align the workings to the planet represented by using a number of systems. The system of Babylonian astrology gives us the days of the week and the hours of the day assigned to each planet. This system is laid out in *The Key of Solomon the King*, which lists days and times for planetary workings (see Table 1 on page 20). You can refer to the *Key of Solomon* to find the best days and times for working the planetary aspects of the Sephiroth.

> It must, therefore, be understood that the Planets have their dominion over the day which approacheth nearest unto the name which is given and attributed unto them, over Saturday, Saturn; Thursday, Jupiter; Tuesday, Mars; Sunday, the Sun; Friday, Venus; Wednesday, Mercury; and Monday, the Moon.
>
> The rule of the Planets over each hour begins from the dawn at the rising of the Sun on the day which takes its name from such Planet, and the Planet which follows it in order, succeeds to the rule over the next hour. Thus (on Saturday) Saturn rules the first hour, Jupiter the second, Mars

Table 1. Daily/Hourly Correspondences of the Sephiroth According to the *Key of Solomon*

Hour of the Day	Saturday Saturn	Sunday Sun	Monday Moon	Tuesday Mars	Wednesday Mercury	Thursday Jupiter	Friday Venus
Dawn	Saturn	Sun	Moon	Mars	Mercury	Jupiter	Venus
Hour 2	Jupiter	Venus	Saturn	Sun	Moon	Mars	Mercury
Hour 3	Mars	Mercury	Jupiter	Venus	Saturn	Sun	Moon
Hour 4	Sun	Moon	Mars	Mercury	Jupiter	Venus	Saturn
Hour 5	Venus	Saturn	Sun	Moon	Mars	Mercury	Jupiter
Hour 6	Mercury	Jupiter	Venus	Saturn	Sun	Moon	Mars
Hour 7	Moon	Mars	Mercury	Jupiter	Venus	Saturn	Sun
Hour 8	Saturn	Sun	Moon	Mars	Mercury	Jupiter	Venus
Hour 9	Jupiter	Venus	Saturn	Sun	Moon	Mars	Mercury
Hour 10	Mars	Mercury	Jupiter	Venus	Saturn	Sun	Moon
Hour 11	Sun	Moon	Mars	Mercury	Jupiter	Venus	Saturn
Hour 12	Venus	Saturn	Sun	Moon	Mars	Mercury	Jupiter
Hour 13	Mercury	Jupiter	Venus	Saturn	Sun	Moon	Mars
Hour 14	Moon	Mars	Mercury	Jupiter	Venus	Saturn	Sun
Hour 15	Saturn	Sun	Moon	Mars	Mercury	Jupiter	Venus
Hour 16	Jupiter	Venus	Saturn	Sun	Moon	Mars	Mercury
Hour 17	Mars	Mercury	Jupiter	Venus	Saturn	Sun	Moon
Hour 18	Sun	Moon	Mars	Mercury	Jupiter	Venus	Saturn
Hour 19	Venus	Saturn	Sun	Moon	Mars	Mercury	Jupiter
Hour 20	Mercury	Jupiter	Venus	Saturn	Sun	Moon	Mars
Hour 21	Moon	Mars	Mercury	Jupiter	Venus	Saturn	Sun
Hour 22	Saturn	Sun	Moon	Mars	Mercury	Jupiter	Venus
Hour 23	Jupiter	Venus	Saturn	Sun	Moon	Mars	Mercury
Hour 24	Mars	Mercury	Jupiter	Venus	Saturn	Sun	Moon

the third, the Sun the fourth, Venus the fifth, Mercury the sixth, the Moon the seventh, and Saturn returns in the rule over the eighth, and the others in their turn, the Planets always keeping the same relative order.

Note that each experiment or magical operation should be performed under the Planet, and usually in the hour, which refers to the same.[1]

Under this system, every planet is represented each day a number of times, and each planet has its own primary day as well (as shown in table 1). For example, if you want to do a Saturn working on Tuesday, find out what time sunrise happens. If the Sun rises at 7 o'clock, the hour from 7 to 8 a.m. is ruled by Mars; 8 to 9 a.m. is ruled by the Sun; 9 to 10 a.m. is ruled by Venus; 10 to 11 a.m. is ruled by Mercury; 11 a.m. to noon is ruled by the Moon; noon to 1 p.m. is ruled by Saturn. So ideally, on Tuesday you would do a Saturn working between noon and 1 p.m. (or, continuing through the day, 7 to 8 p.m.).

While I think this is a good system, I don't want you to get bogged down in the days and times and not do the work because you can't do it according to the chart. Any day and any time is an appropriate time for working a Sephirah.

TAROT CARDS

The knowledge of the Qabalah is contained in the symbols and images of the Tarot.

> We see also what diverse significations are included in the twenty-two Keys which form the universal alphabet of the Tarot, together with the truth of our affirmation, that all secrets of the Qabalah and Magic, all mysteries of the elder world, all science of the patriarchs, all historical traditions of primeval times, are enclosed in this hieroglyphic book of Thoth, Enoch or Cadmus.[2]

In Hermetic magick, Qabalah, the Tarot, and astrological symbolism are intricately connected. To learn and use magical Qabalah, it is necessary to have a solid understanding of the Tarot and a basic knowledge of astrologi-

---

1 S. L. Mathers, *The Key of Solomon the King* (York Beach, ME: Weiser Books, 2000).
2 Eliphas Levi, *Transcendental Magic*, translated by A. E. Waite (York Beach, ME: Weiser Books, 1968).

cal symbolism. While it is not necessary to become an astrologer or to be able to "read" Tarot cards for others, being able to synthesize these systems will aid in your understanding of the Sephiroth.

For each of the Sephirotic exercises, we will use only the numbered Minor Arcana cards. You will review the divinatory meaning for each card pertaining to the Sephirah with which you're working and record this in your journal. If you leave your altar up for a month, you will find it helpful to focus on one card each week. (The Court Cards are not referenced in this work in detail, but they will appear in a later work.)

PERFUMES

When you perform any of the exercises for the Sephiroth, the appropriate Sephirotic incense needs to be burning. If you make your own incense, make enough to last the duration of the working, so there will be aromatic consistency. We will address the appropriate incenses with their corresponding Sephiroth.

Incense-making is one of those tactile things I really enjoy doing. It may also be a task you find rewarding instead of using perfumes purchased in stores. I have created my own incenses for each of the Sephiroth. For herbs and woods, I always mix in a resin base or a fixative. The resin helps bring out the natural aroma and helps remove the "burnt" smell. Grind it up and add the herbs. Grind those together and then burn on charcoal. Use a mortar and pestle; I learned the hard way that you can't grind resins in a coffee grinder. Scents are personal things; that's why there are so many perfumes on the market. Test the incense as you go along, until you get the scent you want. Once you get the desired scent, keep a record of the ingredients and amounts so that you can recreate it as needed.

The incense burner for most of the exercises should be unobtrusive. The censer is a specific magical weapon and we will cover that in a later section. For the Sephirah Yesod, use your big, beautiful, elaborate censer. For all of the other Sephiroth, just use the censer to create scents. You do not want to draw attention to the item itself, so use a smaller, less elaborate vessel for the actual burning of the incense.

MAGICAL WEAPONS

Magical weapons are the most complicated items for you to find and place on the altar. Some are expensive, rare, or difficult to acquire. Some are not even tangible items at all—for instance, the Pain of Obligation. So here is another area in which you need to be creative. It is best to have the actual weapons; but toys, hand-crafted mock-ups, or pictures (again as a last resort) may also suffice. I feel strongly that, over time, a magician should acquire all of the magical weapons and learn to use them for their utilitarian purpose (e.g., learning to shoot a bow and arrow).

Crowley gives some basic information on the description and assignment of the various weapons in *777*. But for most of the magical weapons, we are left to develop our own understanding of the correspondences. Referring to other works, like Crowley's *Book of Thoth* or DuQuette's *Understanding Aleister Crowley's Thoth Tarot,* may help. However, as with all magical work, this is personal and you should develop your own insight into the connection between the Sephirah and its weapon.

CANDLES

While performing the exercises for each of the Sephiroth, burn candles of the Queen Scale color corresponding to the Sephirah you are working. Some of these colors may not be easy to find. For these, you can purchase plain white devotional candles in clear containers and wrap appropriately colored construction paper around the outside.

I purchase all my candles for a dollar or two apiece at a local Catholic supply house. They have a variety of colored glass external holders, plus clear ones that look great with a piece of construction paper wrapped around them. You'll find that candle inserts burn for an extremely long period and are very economical.

RECOMMENDED ALTAR ITEMS

In addition to the items required for your altar, the following items are recommended for inclusion on your altar as well.

Precious Stones

Stones are another tactile representation of the Qabalah. Placing them on your altar gives you more items to experience. By taking them with you and carrying them around during the day, you can have a tiny piece of your altar with you all day. Qabalah can be a joy for all the senses.

Clothing and Apparel

In our daily lives, we understand the power of clothing and the effects it has on our mindset. Imagine a businessman and a surfer. In your mind, you've undoubtedly already imagined them with clothes on, and I wager the businessman is in a suit and tie, while the surfer is wearing shorts and flip-flops. Suits and ties make us feel more professional; shorts and flip-flops make us feel more relaxed and loose. Ritual clothing can also cause a change in your mindset.

You will find it to be a good practice to wear a robe, stole, vestment, or chasuble corresponding to the Sephirah during your working of each of the exercises in this book. These items can be created very easily. Or if you want something more elaborate, they can be purchased from any religious supply store, brick-and-mortar retailer, or Internet specialty shop. There are a variety of ways to adorn yourself in the color of these workings. You can carry a colored handkerchief; wear a pin, earrings, hair ornament, tie, socks, colored scarf, or T-shirt; or you can dye your hair or get some white shirts and dye them. There are a number of ways to wear magical colored items, either conspicuously or inconspicuously, during your working on a daily basis.

Optional Altar Items

The following items are optional and can also be placed on your altar. Their primary use is to further anchor the knowledge of the Sephiroth.

Therefore, only focus on using those that aid you personally in this goal. If the god, animal, or plant doesn't help you understand the Sephirah, don't use it.

There are exercises and information at the end of the book that you can use once you complete the workbook, so that you can go through the Sephiroth again. In subsequent reworking of the Sephiroth, your understanding will deepen and you can add items to your altar. Begin to ask yourself what there is about these items that corresponds to this Sephirah. Knowledge of the Sephiroth is not finite; your capacity and creativity should not be limited either.

God and Goddess Statues

Statues of gods and goddesses corresponding to the Sephiroth can be placed on your altar. For many people, gods are easy and simple reminders of specific qualities—Dionysus is the god of wine, Aphrodite is the goddess of love, etc. These can be used to anchor the concepts and ideas of the Sephiroth more firmly. For each Sephirah, there are a variety of gods and goddesses to choose from. See Appendix B for suggestions on various gods and goddesses to use on your altar. See columns XIX, Selection of Egyptian Gods; XX, Complete Practical Attribution of Egyptian Gods; XXI, The Perfected Man; XXII, Small Selection of Hindu Dieties; XXXIII, Some Scandinavian Gods; XXXIV, Some Greek Gods; XXXV, Some Roman Gods; and XXXVI, Selection of Christian Gods. Only use these if you have a substantial knowledge of the pantheon and if it will aid your understanding of the Sephiroth.

While I do think Crowley had a good grasp of mythology, the columns in *777* dealing with the various pantheons are somewhat lacking. There are many gods and goddesses, as well as many mythologies, missing. For example, I work with Aztec deities, and they are not listed in *777*. So, after much research and study, I made my own Aztec attributions. You may have to wait until after you develop a solid understanding of the Sephiroth before you can ascribe a god or goddess for your personal use.

Animals, Real or Imaginary

Statues or pictures of an animal placed on your altar will suffice. I recommend you draw, paint, or mold them yourself, however. Remember, the object is not to create a work of art that will survive the centuries, only to create something that will anchor you to the Sephiroth. So have fun with it and enjoy *the Labor of Preparation.*

During the working, access to live versions of animals is optimal. For example, go to a zoo or farm, study the animals, pet them, feed them, ride them, and in general spend time experiencing them. Take pictures for your journal.

Plants, Real or Imaginary

Space on any altar is at a premium, so it's not necessary to gather examples of all of the plants associated with a given Sephirah. A small potted plant is ideal as a living, breathing example of the Sephirah. Silk versions of the plants last longer, however, and can be reused in later rituals.

Item Details

Where appropriate, I further explain or give some creative input on certain items for each of the Sephiroth. Remember, however, that this is your altar; it should be something you are comfortable with and more than just a carbon copy of someone else's interpretation (see figure 1).

Figure 1. Yesod altar.

*Please remember: We are not attempting to work the
magical powers of the Sephiroth at this point, only to
learn each Sephirah so that we can eventually work
magically in the Qabalistic universe.*

HOW NOT TO LOSE YOUR MIND

AN ESSAY BY KEITH TAYLOR

y official role in this work has been to serve as Anita's secretary and typist. But in working with her over the last couple of years, I've had the pleasure of actually working through this material. In doing so, I've not only learned a lot about Qabalah, I have also learned what to do and what not to do during this work. I thought I would take a few pages here and share that with you.

SIZE MATTERS

One of the first things I encountered was the disconnect between my eyes and my altar. I began with grandiose plans, huge statues, multiple items for each section, and an itty-bitty altar. On my first altar (Malkuth, as I worked up the Tree the first time), I had two 8-inch statues (one of Gaia and the other of a sphinx), a pomegranate, a branch of ivy, a large bowl of dirt, a small 6-inch triangle and circle, four candles, a large rock crystal, a stole, and the 4 Tens of the Tarot deck. All of this was on an altar just barely large enough to hold everything. Yesod was even worse, and I made it that much worse by switching to a smaller altar as well. For Kether, I actually tried to add a 24-by-36-inch painting on the altar! And this doesn't even address the fact that, after the work is finished for the present, you have to store everything someplace.

I can say that the converse is also true. When working Chokmah, I had the opposite experience. Everything I found happened to be fairly small, so I had a lot of empty space on my altar. After dealing with very cramped and crowded altars up till then, Chokmah seemed lacking. I know it was just psychological, but that didn't stop it from interfering with the work. I managed to rearrange things and place a few more items on the altar to help fill the space better so I could continue without distractions.

When selecting your altar, plan the size based on what you actually want to place on it. If you want large things or lots of them, make sure your altar (and storage area) will hold them comfortably. If you are more practical, then you have the option of going with less space.

Also think about traveling. My job took me all over the United States during my workings, so packing up the altar to take it with me was not practical. I had to make do with setting the wallpaper on my laptop to a photo of my altar, which garnered a lot of interesting looks from clients. Had it been feasible for me to travel with my altar, the sheer size and quantity of my ritual items would have made it impractical to take with me.

IT'S FUN, DAMN IT!

The first interesting thing I picked up during the workings is how much fun gathering up all the altar items can be. Some are obscure, illegal, or non-practical (the plants of Hod come to mind) and some categories have multiple items you can choose from (like the various gods/goddesses). What do you do?

I ended up spending just as much time gathering my altar items as I did for each of the workings. I spent many nights surfing eBay or other shopping sites just to find the "right" item. To me, it became a very elaborate scavenger hunt. Each night, I set out and researched the item or items in question, decided on the general look and feel I wanted, then scoured the Internet trying to find the best match. Most of the time, this took several nights. But when I found the right item, *I found it!* It was as if the universe had led me to the perfect match.

I ended up with some very special items for my altars, each with their own stories and memories that made them that much more special to me. I remember that when they arrived in the mail I ran around screaming, "My new item is here! My new item is here! My new item is here!" like some *jerk*. Because of this, I think I became just as connected to my items during the procurement phase as I did during the working itself.

There were only a handful of items where I did not find exactly what I was truly looking for and had to settle for something else. Again, Hod comes to mind. I would have loved to have moly or *anhalonium lewinii*, but alas they were not legal for me to obtain and I had to settle. So I ended up researching why these were the plants of Hod, what Hodian quality they possessed, and what other plants had that same quality. And I learned from this as well. I'll not tell you what I settled on, so as not to spoil your fun.

KNOW WHEN TO STOP

When I first did this working, I worked from Malkuth upward. I ended up spending a few months on Malkuth—partly because I was enjoying it and partly because I couldn't decide on some of the Yesod altar items. After awhile, I noticed that I had become rather lethargic—I felt literally heavy all the time. I just felt, in general, done. These feelings were so powerful that I felt as if I needed to seek help to understand what had come over me. My life, job, family, etc. were all doing well, so I was having a problem coming to terms with what was happening.

Then, as I was doing some research for another project dealing with astrology, I learned about Saturn and what it represented. The proverbial lightbulb went off in my head, but the dimmer switch had it set to only 50 percent. Still, I felt I was on to something (little did I know!). Again, these feelings were not only emotional; they affected me physically and mentally as well.

I'm not sure how I made the connection, but I just happened upon the Path of Tau, connecting Malkuth and Yesod. Not only did I recognize the Saturn qualities present, but as the Tarot card The Universe, it all began to make sense. Now the dimmer was set to 100—or at least to 90—percent.

I immediately took down the Malkuth altar and set about acquiring the items for Yesod. Within a day, I began to feel the symptoms dissipate and my overall outlook improve. Now I can't say whether I had slipped onto the Path of Tau accidentally, or if I had subconsciously decided I was done with Malkuth and ready to move on. But I do know that I let myself stay there too long.

Ideally, you should work each Sephirah for one month, but this is more of a guideline than a rule. Work each Sephirah for as long as you need to and not a day more or less. Therefore, be very aware of any changes, moods, or feelings you have during each working. Adjust your time in each Sephirah accordingly.

BTW, IT'S NEVER OVER

For each Sephirah, you will most likely find that:

1. You will not be able to obtain a representation of every possible correspondence.

2. Even of those you do obtain, some will leave you more confused than before you started.

Therefore, once you've finished working a Sephirah, just remember that you've only finished your first working of it.

This is especially true if you are only working each Sephirah for a week. There is only so much connection you can gain in a short time with your items and the Sephirah. The more you set up your altars and rework the system, the better connected you become and the more insight you gain. Even if you are working them for a month or more, one go-around is almost a year and, during that year, you'll grow and learn. You may even find that restarting the process with your new self gives you a different look at each Sephirah.

Moreover, I found that, long after I passed from a given Sephirah, I saw things when I was out and about that I thought would be perfect on that altar. So I ended up buying several three-drawer plastic storage containers and setting aside a drawer for each Sephirah and Path. As I found more items that were appropriate for each Sephirah, I bought them and stuck them in the drawers. This not only enhanced my future workings for that Sephirah; it also gave me a magick toolbox for all of my ritual needs.

Whenever I do a ritual for strength and I feel the need to pull out *777*, I find it just as easy and more entertaining to pull out my Gevurah drawer and see what I have. This gives me better inspiration for creating my rituals, and it also serves the practical point of showing me what I actually have on hand to use.

THE REPLACEMENT

777 is a Qabalist's best friend. But let's face it—it's not user-friendly. After doing all of this graphical and tactile work, flipping through *777* eventually became rather boring for me. I found that I really loved the visual aspect of this work. While not actually part of a working, I found that my preliminary research and gathering enriched an already rewarding endeavor (and, no, I'm not paid per word).

My solution to the problem *777* was creating for me was to get a small blank scrapbook from the local hobby store for each Sephirah and fill it with all of the correspondences I uncovered. I printed off images and then wrote a blurb about what that item had in connection to its associated Sephirah. This was especially helpful for items that were completely impossible to obtain (Mr. Hod, I'm talking to you). I also didn't just rely on *777* for the descriptions; I looked at other sources. For instance, for the swan I also researched fairytales like "The Ugly Duckling" and thought about what elements of that story lead the swan to become the animal of Kether.

What I now have are well-organized graphical *777*s that are not only much easier to read, but also more enjoyable.

FINAL THOUGHTS

I hope that what I've offered here in the tales of my successes and failures helps you have a more enjoyable time during your workings. However, my final thoughts on this matter are that you must make this you own working. The way I did this is not the way Anita does this; it's also not the way you're going to do it eventually. Your altar will not look like mine. But that's okay. It's your altar, not mine. As long as you get something out of your altar, then it's a success.

In the end, remember to have fun and enjoy this. Good luck—you'll need it.

THE SEPHIROTH

The *Sefer Yetzirah* is a small book written sometime between the second and fourth centuries. It was part of a larger set of works written by Jewish mystics called the *Ma'aseh Berashith* (In the Beginning). These works come out of the Rabbinical academies that were created after the destruction of the second temple in the first through fourth centuries AD. They consisted of a variety of mystical experiences around the seven heavens (*Hekhaloth*) and the chariot of Ezekiel (*Merkevah*). Within this huge body of work is this little book—*Sefer Yetzirah*—and from this little work we get over a thousand years of mystical and magical hermeneutics.

The Sefer Yetzirah is the method used by God to create the universe. It gives us the term *Sephiroth*. A later work—*Sefer ha-Bahir*—gives us the definition and structure of the Sephiroth. The author of the *Bahir*, which appeared in the eleventh century, is unknown, but the work is the first known writing to apply a "tree" metaphor to the Sephiroth. It is also the first work to assign gender relationships to the Sephiroth and to explore the name of God—the tetragrammaton. In the first chapter of the Sefer Yetzirah, we find this:

> 1. In two and thirty most occult and wonderful paths of wisdom did JAH the Lord of Hosts engrave his name: God of the armies of Israel, ever-living God, merciful and gracious, sublime, dwelling on high, who inhabiteth eternity. He created this universe by the three Sepharim, Number, Writing, and Speech.

2. Ten are the numbers, as are the Sephiroth, and twenty-two the letters, these are the Foundation of all things. Of these letters, three are mothers, seven are double, and twelve are simple.

3. The ten numbers formed from nothing are the decad: these are seen in the fingers of the hands, five on one, five on the other, and over them is the Covenant by voice spiritual, and the rite of Circumcision, corporeal (as of Abraham).

4. Ten are the numbers of the ineffable Sephiroth, ten and not nine, ten and not eleven. Learn this wisdom, and be wise in the understanding of it, investigate these numbers, and draw knowledge from them, fix the design in its purity, and pass from it to its Creator seated on his throne.

5. These Ten Numbers, beyond the Infinite one, have the boundless realms, boundless origin and end, an abyss of good and one of evil, boundless height and depth, East and West, North and South, and the one only God and king, faithful forever seated on his throne, shall rule over all, forever and ever.

6. These ten Sephiroth which are ineffable, whose appearance is like scintillating flames, have no end but are infinite. The word of God is in them as they burst forth, and as they return; they obey the divine command, rushing along as a whirlwind, returning to prostrate themselves at his throne.

7. These ten Sephiroth which are, moreover, ineffable, have their end even as their beginning, conjoined, even as is a flame to a burning coal: for our God is superlative in his unity, and does not permit any second one. And whom canst thou place before the only one?

8. And as to this Decad of the Sephiroth, restrain thy lips from comment, and thy mind from thought of them, and if thy heart fail thee return to thy place; therefore is it written, "The living creatures ran and returned," and on this wise was the covenant made with us.

9. These are the ten emanations of number. One is the Spirit of the Living God, blessed and more than blessed be the name of the Living God of Ages. The Holy Spirit is his Voice, his Spirit, and his Word.[1]

---

1 *Sefer Yetzirah*, translation by William Wynn Westcott, 1893; rpt San Diego: Wizards Bookshelf, 1990.

Qabalah includes many different versions of the Tree of Life and the placement and correspondences of its Paths. In the hermetic tradition, we use the version made popular by Athanasius Kircher and developed by the Golden Dawn. While the Paths have, over time, been arranged and rearranged and their correspondences varied, the Sephiroth have remained, for the most part, consistent. From the *Sefer Yetzirah*—"The Sephiroth are ten in number, no more, no less." While they can be dynamic from an individual perspective, they are static and unchanging with regard to their attributions.

In *Magick in Theory and Practice*, Crowley points out:

> The student must not expect to be given a cut-and-dried definition of what exactly is meant by any of all this. On the contrary, he must work backwards, putting the whole of his mental and moral outfit into these pigeon-holes. You would not expect to be able to buy a filing cabinet with the names of all your past, present and future correspondents ready indexed: your cabinet has a system of letters and numbers meaningless in themselves, but ready to take on a meaning to you, as you fill up the files. As your business increased, each letter and number would receive fresh accessions of meaning for you; and by adopting this orderly arrangement you would be able to have a much more comprehensive grasp of your affairs than would otherwise be the case. By the use of this system the magician is able ultimately to unify the whole of his knowledge—to transmute, even on the Intellectual Plane, the Many into the One.
>
> . . . the true understanding depends entirely upon the work of the Magician himself. Without magical experience it will be meaningless. . . . Let us say, once again, that the magical language is nothing but a convenient system of classification to enable the magician to docket his experiences as he obtains them.
>
> . . . as the student advances in knowledge by experience he will find a progressive subtlety in the magical universe corresponding to his own; for let it be said yet again! not only is his aura a magical mirror of the universe, but the universe is a magical mirror of his aura . . . [2]

Crowley makes some very important points in this edited excerpt from *Magick*. Qabalah is a classification system. At its foundation, we have order—a filing cabinet, as it were—in which to put everything in the universe. It enables us to see connections, correspondences, and relationships,

---

2 Aleister Crowley, *Magick* (York Beach, ME: Weiser Books, 1998), excerpts from pp. 140–143.

and enables us to make order out of chaos so that we can embrace and transcend it. The more the magician studies the universe—Qabalah—the more the magician will know him or herself, in accordance with the dictum: Know thyself.

In general, you may take a number of approaches to working the Sephiroth. You can either start at the top in Kether and work down, or start at the bottom in Malkuth and work up. Each approach teaches you different things and gives you a different perspective. For the purposes of the exercises presented in this book, you will start at Kether and work down toward Malkuth.

The amount of time you spend on each Sephirah and exercise is relative to your ability to integrate the information. I recommend that you spend a minimum of one month on each Sephirah. This may sound like a lot, but understand that you are attempting not just to memorize information, but also to synthesize and integrate it into every level of your magical world. *This takes time.* This work should be both enjoyable and practical, and should not be rushed.

> *Don't skip a Sephirah—*
> *Do them in the order presented!*

CREATING A TREE OF LIFE

The first task is to make a representation of the Tree of Life. There are a variety of ways to do this—as a painting, as a drawing, as a three-dimensional sculpture, etc. My own Tree is on a large piece of Masonite. It is painted flat black, with all the Paths and Sephiroth painted using glossy paint. Create your own unique Tree of Life. Go wherever your creative juices take you. Keith, my

Figure 2. My first Tree of Life.

assistant on the project, made one out of wooden circles and flat wooden sticks. For the workbook, the focus is on the Queen Scale colors from *777,* which you can find in Appendix B. You will find that most other magical books on this topic also use these colors.

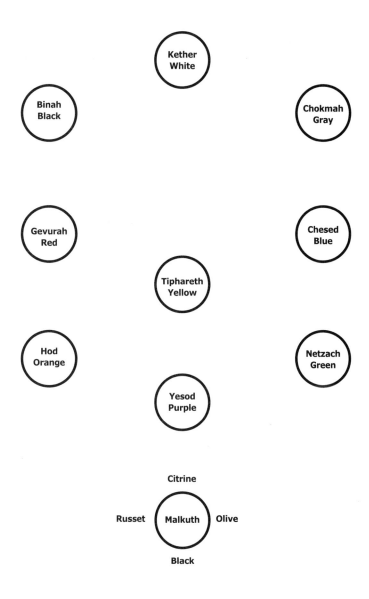

Figure 3. A basic Tree of Life.

You can reference the cover of the book to see an example, and there are examples given in figures 2 and 3. The purpose of this exercise is to give you a physical, tactile representation of the Tree of Life. Be creative, but keep it simple. Don't write any information on your Tree yet, just keep it to colors for the moment.

THE
SUPERNAL
TRIAD

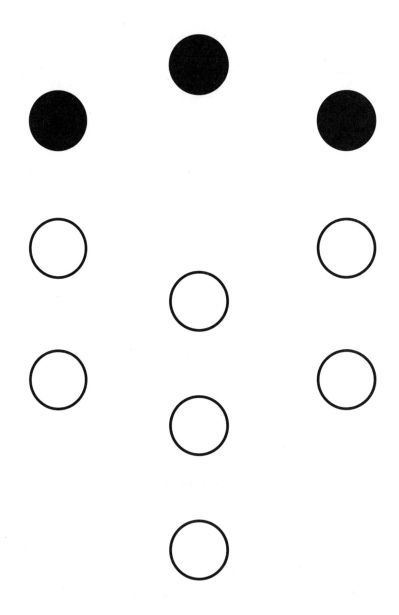

Figure 4. The Supernal Triad.

THE FIRST THREE SEPHIROTH are called the Supernals. They exist above the abyss. They exist as a unity and are not to be thought of individually. We live in a world that understands and functions with ideas like right and wrong, left and right, up and down, black and white. The Supernals exist beyond these concepts. They are always in union; consequently, in Jewish Qalabah, to work Chokmah and Binah individually is to sin. There is no division here. The Supernals transcend all concepts of opposites or difference. In *Magick in Theory and Practice* (Book IV, Part III) Crowley continues his basic outline of the Qabalistic universe. Beginning with the Supernal Triad he states:

THE MAGICAL THEORY
OF THE UNIVERSE

There are three main theories of the universe; Dualism, Monism, and Nihilism. It is impossible to enter into a discussion of their relative merits in a popular manual of this sort. They may be studied in Erdmann's *History of Philosophy* and similar treatises. All are reconciled and unified in the theory which we shall now set forth . . .

Infinite space is called the goddess NUIT, while the infinitely small and atomic yet omnipresent point is called HADIT. . . . These are unmanifest. One conjunction of these infinites is called RA-HOOR-KHUIT, more correctly, HERU-RA-HA, to include HOOR-PAAR-KRAAT, a unity which includes and heads all things. . . .

Unity transcends *consciousness*. It is above all division. The Father of thought—the Word—is called Chaos—the dyad. The number Three, the Mother, is called Babalon. . . . This first triad is essentially unity, in a manner transcending reason. The comprehension of this Trinity is a matter of spiritual experience. All true gods are attributed to this Trinity.[1]

The names of the Sephiroth come from the *Sefer ha-Bahir*, and are taken from the Torah. The Supernals—Kether, Chokmah, and Binah—are from Exodus 31: 3:

> Then the Lord said to Moses, "See, I have chosen Bezalel son of Uri, the son of Hur, of the tribe of Judah, and I have filled him with the Spirit of God [Kether], with wisdom,[Chokmah] with understanding, [Binah] with knowledge [Daath] and with all kinds of skills—to make artistic designs for work in gold, silver and bronze, to cut and set stones, to work in wood, and to engage in all kinds of crafts."

Each Sephirah in the Supernal Triad is unique. They have their own attributions, words, entities, and meanings. We will study them separately, but will work Chokmah and Binah together.

ASTROLOGY, TAROT, AND THE SUPERNAL TRIAD

The zodiac can be organized into a number of groupings. The two we will use are elements and triplicities. Each sign is associated with an element and a triplicity. The triplicities are the Cardinal, Fixed, and Mutable signs; the elements are Fire, Water, Air, and Earth. Each Minor Arcana Tarot card is associated with a zodiacal sign. Bear with me, this is not as complicated as it first may seem.

The zodiac is a wheel that has 360 degrees broken into twelve signs of 30 degrees each. So Aries has 30 degrees of the wheel, Taurus has 30 degrees, and so on. Each degree represents roughly one day (the year having 365 rather than 360 days means that it's not a perfect representation).

Kether—the first Sephirah on the Tree of Life—represents the elements in their purest form. Kether exists before the zodiac and is not rep-

---

1 Crowley, *Magick*, pp. 137–138.

resented in the zodiacal wheel. Kether contains the elements before they explode into creation, compact and intense. It is represented by the Aces of the Tarot.

The Cardinal signs are in the second and third Sephiroth of the Supernal Triad, Chokmah and Binah, and in the fourth Sephirah, Chesed (see figure 5). The Cardinal signs represent the cardinal points of a compass—east, north, west, and south—and/or the cycle of a year—spring, summer, fall, and winter—and/or the cycle of a day—sunrise, midnight, sunset, and noon (see table 2 on page 46). Cardinal signs are the initial explosion of the element; they are the element at its moment of creation—their own "Big Bang," as it were. They are Aries/Fire, Cancer/Water, Libra/Air, and Capricorn/Earth.

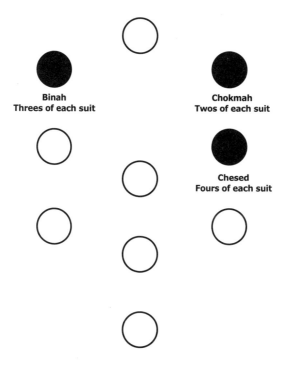

Figure 5. The Cardinal signs. The Three Sephiroth associated with the Cardinal Signs, Aries, Cancer, Libra, and Capricorn.

Table 2. The Cardinal Signs and Their Associations

Signs								
Aries	Fire	Wands	Beginning of spring	East	Sunrise	1–10°	Two of Wands	Chokmah
						11–20°	Three of Wands	Binah
						21–30°	Four of Wands	Chesed
Cancer	Water	Cups	Beginning of summer	North	Midnight	1–10°	Two of Cups	Chokmah
						11–20°	Three of Cups	Binah
						21–30°	Four of Cups	Chesed
Libra	Air	Swords	Beginning of fall	West	Sunset	1–10°	Two of Swords	Chokmah
						11–20°	Three of Swords	Binah
						21–30°	Four of Swords	Chesed
Capricorn	Earth	Disks	Beginning of winter	South	Noon	1–10°	Two of Disks	Chokmah
						11–20°	Three of Disks	Binah
						21–30°	Four of Disks	Chesed

Each of the Minor Arcana cards, numbers Two through Ten, represents 10 degrees of a zodiacal sign. The Twos, Threes, and Fours are the Cardinal signs. For example, the Two of Wands represents Aries degrees 1 through 10; the Three of Wands is Aries degrees 11 through 20; the Four of Wands is Aries degrees 21 through 30.

The Cardinal signs and associations are:

```
                              │ Capricorn
                              │ Earth
                              │ Disks
                              │ Winter
                              │ Noon*
Aries                         │ South                    Libra
Fire                          │                          Air
Wands                         │                          Swords
Spring      ──────────────────┼──────────────────        Fall
Sunset                        │                          Sunset
East                          │                          West
                              │
                              │ Cancer
                              │ Water
                              │ Cups
                              │ Summer
                              │ Midnight*
                              │ North
```

Within the Supernal Triad, we have the initial elements and the first explosion or initiation of the elements in Chokmah and Binah. Understanding the Cardinal signs and the Minor Arcana cards will help develop your insight into each Sephirah.

*Midnight and noon can be either those times based on a clock or the positions of the Sun in the sky, which is what I prefer. Noon is when the Sun is directly overhead; midnight is when the night is the darkest.

KETHER—CROWN
כתר

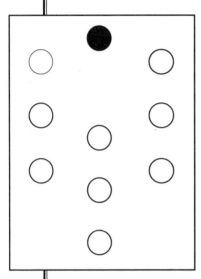

Color: White brilliance

Zodiacal and Planetary Representation: Sphere of the *Primum Mobile* (Big Bang, all of reality, puts everything in motion)

Tarot Cards: The 4 Aces—Wands, Cups, Swords, Disks

Perfume: Ambergris

Magical Weapons: Swastika or Fylfot Cross, Crown, Lamp

Precious Stone: Diamond

God or Goddess Statues: Jupiter (Roman), Zeus (Greek), Ptah (Egyptian)

Animals, Real or Imaginary: God, Hawk, Swan

Plants, Real or Imaginary: Almond in flower, Banyan Tree

Magical Power: Union with God

Additional Associations: Crown, the most hidden of all hidden things; the point, absolute compassion, primal stirrings of intent, the arousal of desire, the origin of will; air that cannot be grasped, the hidden light, the Ancient Holy One.

The Sephirah of Kether is the first emanation on the Tree of Life. Kether means crown. This is exemplified by the crowns in the 4 Aces of the Tarot. As Crowley states in *777*, Kether is primarily the individual point of view. It is the "I AM" moment. As Malkuth is the culmination of all things above it, Kether is the beginning of all things below it.

ACQUIRE AND FURNISH YOUR ALTAR

Zodiacal and Planetary Representation and the Tarot Cards

Kether is represented by the Sphere of the *Primum Mobile*, which is considered all of reality or the first cause that is the moment just before the Big Bang. It is the point that puts everything in motion. Crowley represented Kether as the god Ra-Hoor-Khuit.

- What do you think is a good representation of all of reality, or the point that becomes the Big Bang?

Tarot

- Place the 4 Aces on your altar.

Perfume

The perfume of Kether is ambergris. Basically, ambergris is sperm-whale vomit. It was used as a fixative in perfumes because it helps other fragrances hold their scents. Once ambergris dries, ages, and is heated, it takes on an earthy scent. It was believed to have been used by Cleopatra to lure Marc Anthony, and by the wife of Alexander the Great to remind him of what he had waiting at home. It shows up in many other stories and mythologies as well.

Ambergris is known as "sailor's gold." It's very expensive. Recently, a woman in South Africa found a chunk on the beach and it brought her $300,000. Because ambergris is so costly, it is usually replaced in perfumery with a synthetic version. Ambergris is used today in lots of perfumes, including ones by Michael Kors and Dolce & Gabbana. I can't confirm whether they use synthetic or raw ambergris. The perfume *Eau de Merveilles* by the French firm Hermès. claims to use raw ambergris.

Ambergris is associated with Kether because it is also associated with the divinity of kings and queens and is recognized for its power over men. As a fixative, its power comes in unifying many scents into one scent.

- Research ambergris.

- What additional information did you discover?

- Why do you think ambergris is the perfume of Kether?

Magical Weapons

In my opinion, the swastika as a symbol, even when drawn correctly, has been successfully co-opted by the Nazis. If you can use the symbol without images of Hitler entering your mind, then go ahead. Otherwise, I suggest using a different weapon.

The crown is the weapon of royalty. It is the representation of "supreme deity which the magician assumes." In *Magick* (Book IV, Part II, Chapter XI), Crowley tells us:

> The Crown of the Magician represents the Attainment of his Work. It is a band of pure gold, on the front of which stand three pentagrams, and on the back a hexagram. The central pentagram contains a diamond or a great opal; the other three symbols contain the Tau. Around this Crown is twined the golden Uraeus serpent, with erect head and expanded hood. Under the Crown is a crimson cap of maintenance, which falls to the shoulders.[2]

Crowley also gives a great description of a crown in the Gnostic Mass:

> The crown may be of gold or platinum, or of electrum magicum; but with no other metals, save the small proportions necessary to a proper alloy. It may be adorned with divers jewels, at will. But it must have the Uraeus serpent twined about it, and the cap of maintenance must match the scarlet of the Robe. Its texture should be velvet.[3]

---

2 Crowley, *Magick*, p. 104.
3 Crowley, *Magick*, p. 587.

- Procure your crown. This can be an ongoing process. Most people can't afford a gold crown right away. Journal about your crown.

The lamp is listed as one of the magical weapons of Kether; however, the lamp itself is not the weapon. The weapon is rather the light that comes from the lamp; it represents the light descending. Your lamp can be an oil lamp or an electric one.[4]

- What type of lamp did you choose and why?

Precious Stone

The diamond is the stone of Kether. It is pure compressed carbon and, as Crowley points out, the base element for all life. Get a diamond for your altar—preferably a cut diamond, not a raw one. It can be a chip and doesn't have to be set in any jewelry. Borrow one if you have to, but get a real diamond, not a cubic zirconia.

- Research how natural diamonds are made. Journal!

- Why is the diamond the gemstone of Kether?

Clothing and Apparel

Unlike the other Sephiroth (which you'll find out soon enough), Kether workings are ideally performed in the nude, with the exception of a crown. Start out with nothing on your body that you were not born with—at least to the extent possible. You may consider covering tattoos with some masking makeup, taking off jewelry, and viewing your body in its simplest form.

---

4   Suggested additional reading, Aleister Crowley, *Magick,* Book IV, Part II, chapter X, "The Lamp."

Animals, Real or Imaginary

Thelemites may find that a hawk is more memorable and significant on the altar. You can also place a mirror on your altar to look into and see the face of God, your true divinity.

- Research the hawk and the swan. Journal any information that you perceive is relevant to Kether.

Plants, Real or Imaginary

The banyan tree is a fig tree and is perfect for Kether. The tree starts as a seed up in a host tree and grows down until its roots grow into the ground. It thus gives the appearance of multiple trunks, but in fact it is one tree. You can find a lot of great information on the banyan tree in the Bhagavad Gita. In Hinduism, it is considered a sin to destroy a banyan tree, and it is also considered commendable to plant a new one, as well as a bodhi tree.

- If you can find a banyan tree, either in the wild or at an arboretum, spend some time meditating under its branches. If you can't, look up images of the banyan.

The almond in flower is a little more straightforward. The Staff of Aaron, the staff that Moses used in Egypt to bring down the ten plagues, was made from an almond branch in flower. It was later passed on to Joshua and finally placed in the Ark of the Covenant with the plate of manna and the stone tablets of Moses. When the people were good, the staff produced edible sweet almonds. When they sinned, it produced poisonous bitter almonds. Almond flowers are also used to represent the virgin birth of Jesus and as a symbol of Mary. The almond in the United States is grown primarily in California, but it is easy to grow.

- Research both banyan and almond trees, as well as almond flowers. Journal anything that adds to your understanding of these two trees and Kether.

STUDY YOUR ALTAR

Once your Sephirotic altar is complete and ready for use, set aside time every day and perform the following exercises (at least once a day, but the more time you can spare the better). At this point, the exact time you choose is up to you.

The goal of these exercises is to help you learn each Sephirah and to understand its correspondences. This will aid you not only in each of the remaining exercises, but also throughout your Qabalistic workings.

- Light or turn on the lamp. Focus on the light that the lamp brings into the room. Observe the intensity of the light as it moves farther away from its source. Note how it fades, creates shadows. Note the places in the room, even around the altar, where the light doesn't reach.

While this may seem simple, the point is to understand that the light of Kether fades as it descends. And even in its descent, things are not always as they seem. Divine light is blocked and changed by the things it encounters. While the light shines brightly, it causes areas of equally intense darkness when it encounters anything.

- Light your incense. Close your eyes and breathe in the aroma. Let the scent take you to your altar.

- Study the Kether altar intently.

- Move things around on the altar to facilitate other connections between items on the altar.

- Allow the word *Kether* (Crown) to repeat itself in your mind.

- Pick up the items on your altar and understand them. Remind yourself why each item is on the Kether altar.

- If you chose a god or a goddess to place on your altar, journal why this deity is appropriate to Kether. What about the deity connects you to Kether?

- Look at each item and journal why you think each one is appropriate on the Kether altar.

- Sometimes, the correspondences do not necessarily correlate to each other. Are there items on the altar that do not seem to relate to each other, even though they relate to Kether?

KETHER, THE ZODIAC, AND THE TAROT[5]

Study each of the Ace cards individually, in the following order: Wands (Fire), Cups (Water), Swords (Air), and Disks (Earth).

- Spend time contemplating each one and how it is related to Kether.

- What is the divinatory meaning of each card and how does Kether influence this meaning?

- As you go through the exercises, you can and should develop your own understanding and meaning of each card based on your insights. How does your understanding of Kether change your personal understanding of the cards?

- If you are doing the exercises for Kether for an entire month, consider focusing on one Tarot card each week.

KETHER—CROWN (כתר)

The divine name for Kether is אהיה (Eheieh), which means "I am" in Hebrew. When Moses asked God by what name he should refer to Him, God responded אהיה.

---

5   Suggested additional reading, Lon Milo DuQuette, *Understanding Aleister Crowley's Thoth Tarot* (York Beach, ME: Weiser Books, 2003), chapter 17, "The Four Aces."

Now Moses said to God, "Suppose I go to the Israelites and say to them, 'The God of your fathers has sent me to you,' and they ask me, 'What is his name?' Then what shall I tell them?"

God said to Moses, "I AM WHO I AM. This is what you are to say to the Israelites: 'I AM has sent me to you.'" [6]

- Take time every day to be nude in front of a mirror large enough to see your entire body. This is the time to reflect on the concept of existence.

- As you look at your body, say אהיה—"I am." Your mind will naturally want to add words after this statement—I am woman; I am man; I am teacher, lawyer, boyfriend, wife, etc. Try to get your mind to just the *I am*. Just *be* in the moment. Journal all of the words that come after the "I am" initially.

- Write your own description of Kether. Let your thoughts and feelings flow. Do not worry about whether you are right or wrong; just write what comes to you and what seems Kether-like to you.

ADDITIONAL CORRESPONDENCES

Now that you have developed a better understanding of Kether, let's move beyond *777* to create your own correspondences. There are two senses not addressed by *777*. One is taste; the other is sound.

- Choose a food based on your understanding of Kether. A food that is essential to every other recipe—salt—is what I use. I can't think of any other food or spice or condiment that is in every item we eat and drink in some form or another and that is essential to life at a basic level.

---

6   Exodus 3:13–14.

- Choose a song or type of music. You may select songs from different genres (classical, rock, etc.) and have multiple columns, as in the god and goddess columns in Appendix B.

- Continue this with other categories—occupations, drinks, movies, etc. (*The Wizard of Oz* is a particularly interesting and entertaining movie for this purpose). Add these categories to your own *777* chart in Appendix B and use these same categories throughout the Sephiroth.

For the first five years of a local festival during the Saturday night fire, I bartended the Qabalah Bar. A female let us draw the Tree of Life on her body and she then lay down and became the bar itself. Each Sephirah was then assigned a specific alcohol. I selected various alcohols that I felt appropriately correlated with each Sephirah and, as people came up, I gave them a quick Qabalah lesson (if necessary) and they selected a drink based on the Sephirah they wanted to invoke for the night. I served them that alcohol in a shot cup. It's one of my favorite Qabalah classes and lots of fun coming up with the correspondences.

Please log on to the website www.magickqabalah.com *and let us know what you come up with. I would love to hear about other thoughts regarding this.*

Remember, you will be returning to these exercises later in the workbook, so be sure to journal your experiences, thoughts, visions, and feelings. You don't always have to write essays. You can draw pictures, doodle, and use photography. Find a method of journaling your experiences that works for you.

CHOKMAH—WISDOM
חכמה

Color: Gray

Zodiacal and Planetary Representation: Sphere of the Zodiac

Tarot Cards: The 4 Twos—Dominion (Wands), Love (Cups), Peace (Swords), Change (Disks)

Perfume: Musk

Magical Weapons: Linga, Inner Robe of Glory; The Word or *Logos* (in written form), Wand or Hollow Tube.

Precious Stones: Star Ruby, Turquoise

God or Goddess Statues: Janus (Roman), Athena (Greek), Amoun (Egyptian)

Animal, Real or Imaginary: Man

Plants, Real or Imaginary: Amaranth, Mistletoe, Pipal Tree (Bodhi Tree, sacred fig tree, also known by a number of other names)

Magical Power: Vision of God

Additional Associations: Wisdom, beginning, origin, seed, will, line without shape, father, lingham, active force.

The Sephirah of Chokmah is the second emanation on the Tree of Life. Chokmah is the wisdom that comes with the first ray of the light. It is the first thing the mind can grasp.

In Qabalah, it is impossible to work in Binah and Chokmah separately, since there is no division above the abyss. However, we are not working the Sephiroth, only learning about them, so we will initially take each one individually.

ACQUIRE AND FURNISH YOUR ALTAR

Zodiacal and Planetary Representation and the Tarot Cards

Chokmah contains all of the stars of the zodiac. There are many ways to represent the zodiac. You can make a sash or stole with the signs of the zodiac on it. You can run your natal chart and place that on your altar. Find a way to represent the zodiac; be creative!

- While Chokmah contains the entire zodiac, it is also represented by the Cardinal signs—Aries, Cancer, Libra, and Capricorn. The first 10 degrees of each sign correspond to the Twos of each suit of the tarot.

- Place the 4 Twos on your altar—Dominion, Love, Peace, and Change.

Perfume

The perfume of Chokmah is musk. Musk has an interesting history, having been used since ancient times in perfumes and incenses. The word "musk" comes from the Sanskrit *muska,* which means testicles. Musk is therefore an obvious scent for Chokmah. Today, musk is primarily synthetic, since extracting it from animals involves killing the animal. You may acquire real musk, but it is extremely expensive—three times more expensive than gold. Many perfumes on the market, however, use "white musk," the synthetic equivalent. These are not cheap either, but they are more affordable than real musk.

- Research musk; journal.

Magical Weapons

The linga is one of the magical weapons of Chokmah; it represents the male creative force or phallus. If you can, get a linga-yoni, which symbolizes the joining of Chokmah and Binah, or draw or paint a linga. Place only your linga on your altar.

- If you have a *linga*, you can take a picture of it or make a sculpture of your linga, phallus, or male generative power.

The Inner Robe of Glory is the second weapon ascribed to Chokmah. The Inner Robe is the Yod, the straight line, the uplifted rod.[7]

The word (or *logos*) has a number of meanings depending on the time period. It was used by Aristotle, Socrates, and other philosophers, but it was also commandeered by Christianity.

- Research the word *logos* and take notes. Journal.

- Decide which aspects best fit in your understanding of Chokmah.

In Jewish Qabalah, the logos of Chokmah is the written Torah, while the logos of Binah is the oral tradition of Qabalah. Both were given to Moses on Mount Sinai.

- How would you translate the logos into a practical magical weapon?

---

7 Suggested additional reading, *The Hymn of the Robe of Glory,* translated by G. R. S. Mead (available online). Pay special attention to his notes and descriptions. It is a beautiful poem and his commentary is exemplary. Don't try to understand the whole thing in your reading, only glean from it a better understanding of the Robe of Glory. What did you take from the poem? How did it influence your understanding of the Inner Robe of Glory? Record these thoughts in your journal.

In *Magick in Theory and Practice,* Crowley identifies that "One Word" that becomes your word, the foundation of your religion or true will.

> One must find out for oneself, and make sure beyond doubt, *who* one is, *what* one is, *why* one is. This done, one may put the will which is implicit in the "why" into words, or rather into One Word. Being thus conscious of the proper course to pursue, the next thing is to understand the conditions necessary to following it out.[8]

Precious Stone

The star ruby, Crowley says, represents the male energy of the creative star. It's a beautiful, light-red stone with a white star emanating out from the middle, much like a star sapphire. If you cannot get a star ruby, look it up online or go into a jewelry store and study one.

Turquoise, according to Crowley, represents Mazloth, which means "constellations." This seems appropriate, as Chokmah is the entire zodiac.

Animal, Real or Imaginary

Man is the only animal Crowley suggests for Chokmah. If you select a statue of a male for this altar, don't select one that represents a god. Select a statue of a plain male that can represent all men. For this purpose, a generic statue is better I think. If you are male or self-identify as a male, then I suggest a mirror, so that you can look into the mirror and understand your personal connection to Chokmah.

- Can you come up with another animal, real or imaginary, that may be appropriate for Chokmah?

- One suggestion from our local group is the stag. What are your thoughts on this? Is this an appropriate choice?

- Record these thoughts in your journal.

---

8   Crowley, *Magick,* p. 134.

Plants, Real or Imaginary

Amaranth and mistletoe both represent immortality. They are the hiding place of the Sun in old myths of winter. They are alive when all other things seemingly die. The pipal tree is the tree that the Buddha sat under during his quest for enlightenment. It is the tree of enlightenment.

- Research amaranth, mistletoe, and the pipal tree. Journal.

Depending on where you live, all of these are great representations for your altar. Growing a fig tree, or perhaps partaking of some figs, can also work.

STUDY YOUR ALTAR

Once your Sephirotic altar is complete and ready for use, set aside time every day and perform the following exercises (at least once a day, but the more time you can spare the better). The time you choose is up to you.

- Light your incense. Close your eyes and breathe in the aroma. Let the scent take you to your altar.

- Study the Chokmah altar intently.

- Move things around on the altar to facilitate other connections between items on the altar.

- Allow the word *Chokmah* (Wisdom) to repeat itself in your mind.

- Pick up the items on your altar and understand them. Remind yourself why each item is on the Chokmah altar.

- If you chose a god or goddess to place on your altar, journal why this deity is appropriate to Chokmah. What about the deity connects you to Chokmah?

- Look at each item and journal why you think each one is appropriate on the Chokmah altar.

- Sometimes, the correspondences do not necessarily correlate to each other. Are there items on the altar that do not seem to relate to each other, even though they relate to Chokmah?

- Pick up your statue of the man, or look into the mirror. Think about the male generative force.

- Pick up the linga. How do you perceive the male generative force? Journal.

- Focus on wisdom. Why do you think the light gives us wisdom first?

CHOKMAH, THE ZODIAC, AND THE TAROT[9]

Study each of the Two cards of the Tarot individually, in the following order: Wands—Dominion (Fire), Cups—Love (Water), Swords—Peace (Air), and Disks—Change (Earth).

- Chokmah contains Cardinal signs. Cardinal signs are the pivotal point; they are the hinge of the seasons, the moment of change, the explosion from spring to summer, summer to fall, dark of night to first light of day. How do the Cardinal aspects manifest in Chokmah?

- Spend time contemplating each card and how it is related to Chokmah.

- What is the divinatory meaning of each card and how does Chokmah influence this meaning?

---

9 Suggested additional reading, Lon Milo DuQuette, *Understanding Aleister Crowley's Thoth Tarot* (York Beach, ME: Weiser Books, 2003), chapter 19, "The Small Cards," up to the description of each card individually, then read each section pertaining to the cards listed in this section only.

- As you go through the exercises, you can and should develop your own understanding and meaning of each card based on your insights. How does your understanding of Chokmah change your personal understanding of the cards?

- If you are doing the exercises for Chokmah for an entire month, consider doing one Tarot card each week.

CHOKMAH—WISDOM (חכמה)

Chokmah means "wisdom" in Hebrew. Think about what wisdom means to you.

- Who is the wisest person you know?

- What is it about the person that makes him or her wise?

- How does the person show his or her wisdom?

- List examples of times when you were wise.

- Reflect on why you were able to project and use wisdom in these situations.

- Think of someone who is really lacking in wisdom.

- What behaviors show that this person lacks this quality?

- Florence Farr's Golden Dawn magical motto was *Sapientia Sapienti Dono Data* (Wisdom is a gift, given to the wise). What do you think this means?

- Read the *Apology* by Plato. It is a short work available on the Internet. In particular, under Socrates' Defense, he discusses wisdom, both his and others'. Socrates says:

For when I heard this, I reasoned thus with myself, What does the god mean? What enigma is this? For I am not conscious to myself that I am wise, either much or little.

- In *Liber Librae, The Book of Balance*, the author (probably Samuel Liddell MacGregor Mathers) states:

He who knoweth little thinketh he knoweth much, but he who knoweth much hath learned his own ignorance.[10]

- What do you think Socrates and Mathers meant by these statements?

ADDITIONAL CORRESPONDENCES

Now that you have developed a better understanding of Chokmah, you can move beyond *777* to create your own correspondences. There are two senses not addressed by *777*. One is taste; the other is sound.

- Choose a food based on your understanding of Chokmah.

- Choose a song or type of music. You can select songs from different genres (classical, rock, etc.) and have multiple columns, like the *777* chart in Appendix B.

- Continue this with other categories—occupations, drinks, movies, etc. Add these categories to your own *777* chart in Appendix B and use these same categories throughout the Sephiroth.

---

10 Crowley, *Magick*, p. 668.

BINAH—UNDERSTANDING
בינה

Color: Black

Zodiacal and Planetary Representation: Sphere of Saturn ♄

Tarot Cards: The 4 Threes—Virtue (Wands), Abundance (Cups), Sorrow (Swords), Work (Disks)

Perfumes: Myrrh, Civet

Magical Weapons: Yoni, Outer Robe of Concealment, Cup (In Jewish tradition the *logos* as the oral word of God is associated with Binah.)

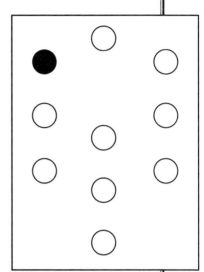

Precious Stones: Star Sapphire, Pearl

God or Goddess Statues: Juno (Roman), Demeter (Greek), Maut (Egyptian)

Animals, Real or Imaginary: Woman, Bee

Plants, Real or Imaginary: Cypress, Opium Poppy

Magical Powers: Vision of Sorrow

Additional Associations: Understanding, spring, mother, contemplation, palace of mirrors, wife, womb, palace, vows, oral *logos*.

The Sephirah of Binah is the third emanation on the Tree of Life. Binah is the understanding that comes with experience of something. Binah is the mother; she is the force that, along with the wisdom of Chokmah, brings about manifestation.

ACQUIRE AND FURNISH YOUR ALTAR

Zodiacal and Planetary Representation and the Tarot

- Research the zodiacal planet Saturn.

- Binah is the second 10 degrees of each of the Cardinal signs—Aries, Cancer, Libra, and Capricorn—and the Threes of each Tarot suit. Place the 4 Threes on your altar—Virtue, Abundance, Sorrow, and Work.

Perfumes

The perfumes of Binah are myrrh or civet, a musk extracted from a small mammal by that name native to Asia and Africa. Because extracting the musk requires killing the civet, a synthetic civet musk is produced by Chanel and is the scent of Chanel No. 5.

- Research myrrh and civet. Journal.

Magical Weapons

The yoni is the female generative power or genitalia. There are lots of things you can do for this.

- If you procured a linga-yoni for your Chokmah altar, place only the yoni part on your Binah altar.

- If you have a *yoni*, you can take a yoni picture for your altar.

- If you do not possess a yoni, paint or draw a picture of one.

> *I was at a temple some years ago where the local group of women had made yoni pictures. They covered their yonis in paint and then straddled a piece of paper on a curved surface. When they stood up, they had beautiful pictures. They were hung all around the room and it took a while for me to figure out what they were.*

A fountain is another excellent representation of the yoni, symbolizing the free-flowing waters of Binah. The waters of Malkuth, the tenth emanation, are closed up in a well; at this point, the waters are open and flow freely.

The Outer Robe of Concealment refers to the darkness of Binah. Binah is the mother. It is the darkness before birth into the light. Think about a pregnant woman; she is the Outer Robe of Concealment. She conceals a potential new life in a safe, dark place. At birth, the babe descends into the light to take a breath of air, whereat the babe's lungs begin processing oxygen and its blood turns red; its heart pumps blood to the lungs to get that oxygen. The babe begins to eat and use its digestive system completely.

However, while in the Robe of Concealment, the babe has developed emotionally. It can cry, express emotions, hear, and process information. So, while birth into the light brings a child into manifestation, within the Robe, that child has already begun the journey of wisdom and understanding. If you happen to be pregnant, this is a good time to reflect on your role as mother, on the life you conceal.

While it's clear that the Inner Robe and Outer Robe have a deeper esoteric meaning, one could symbolize these by creating a robe whose inside is lined in a luxurious material experienced and known only by the magician, while the external or visible robe is simple cotton or wool. Or make the Robe as Crowley describes in *Magick* (Book IV, Part II, Chapter XII). Making a robe is very easy. I suggest that, if you don't make it yourself, you should at least assist the person making it.

Crowley adds the Cup to the list in the column explanations. I certainly agree and this is a great time to acquire a magical cup. In *Magick* (Book II, Chapter VII), Crowley states:

> As the Magick Wand is the Will, the Wisdom, the Word of the Magician, so is the Magick Cup his Understanding. . . .
>
> And it is also the cup in the hand of OUR LADY BABALON, and the cup of the Sacrament.
>
> This Cup is full of bitterness, and of blood, and of intoxication.
>
> The Understanding of the Magus is his link with the Invisible, on the passive side.
>
> His Will errs actively by opposing itself to the Universal Will.
>
> His Understanding errs passively when it receives influence from that which is not the ultimate truth.[11]

Precious Stones

Crowley describes the star sapphire as a star in the blue sky whose light goes on infinitely. You can see this if you look at a genuine star sapphire. The star in the middle seems to beam out from the stone.

The pearl was added later by Crowley:

> The Pearl is referred to Binah on account of its being the typical stone of the sea. It is formed by concentric spheres of hard brilliant substance, the centre being a particle of dust. Thus, that dust which is all that remains of the Exempt Adept after he has crossed the Abyss, is gradually surrounded by sphere after sphere of shining splendour, so that he becomes a fitting ornament for the bosom of the Great Mother.[12]

Why do you think Crowley adds the pearl as a stone of Binah?

---

11 Crowley, *Magick*, p. 73.
12 Crowley, *Magick*, p. 102.

Animals, Real or Imaginary

If you select a statue of a female for this altar, don't select one that pertains to a goddess. Select a statue of a plain female; a pregnant one would be appropriate. Since the statue represents all women, a generic statue is a better choice than a specific one. If you are a female or self-identify as a female, I suggest a mirror, so that you can look into the mirror and understand your personal connection to Binah.

In the columns explanation on Animals in *777*, Crowley adds the bee. The bee is a representation of the yoni by virtue of its shape. However, I believe the queen bee is appropriate for Binah as well, by virtue of its purpose and activity.

- Research the bee. Journal.

Plants, Real or Imaginary

Cypress is the plant of Saturn. Opium poppy is an interesting choice here. Opium has traditionally been associated with inspiration. Poppies are bright beautiful flowers with a chocolatey scent, whose seeds are intoxicating and make one fall into a dreamlike opiate state.

- Research cypress and opium poppy. Journal.

STUDY YOUR ALTAR

Once your Sephirotic altar is complete and ready for use, set aside time every day and perform the following exercises (at least once a day, but the more time you can spare the better). The time you choose is up to you. It's good to do the Binah workings in the dark if possible.

- Light your incense. Close your eyes and breathe in the aroma. Let the scent take you to your altar.

- Study the Binah altar intently.

- Move things around on the altar to facilitate other connections between items on the altar.

- Allow the word *Binah* (Understanding) to repeat itself in your mind.

- Pick up the items on your altar and understand them. Remind yourself why each item is on the Binah altar.

- If you chose a god or goddess to place on your altar, journal why this deity is appropriate to Binah. What about the deity connects you to Binah?

- Look at each item and journal why you think each one is appropriate on the Binah altar.

- Sometimes, the correspondences do not necessarily correlate to each other. Are there items on the altar that do not seem to relate to each other, even though they relate to Binah?

BINAH, THE ZODIAC, AND THE TAROT[13]

Study each of the Three cards individually, in the following order: Wands—Virtue (Fire), Cups—Abundance (Water), Swords—Sorrow (Air), and Disks—Work (Earth).

- The planet Saturn manifests in Binah. What about Saturn's attributions suggests Binah?

- Cardinal signs also manifest in Binah, as well as in Chokmah. How do the Cardinal aspects manifest in Binah?

- Spend time contemplating each card and how it is related to Binah.

---

13 Suggested additional reading, Lon Milo DuQuette, *Understanding Aleister Crowley's Thoth Tarot* (York Beach, ME: Weiser Books, 2003), chapter 19, "The Small Cards," up to the description of each card individually, then read each section pertaining to the cards listed in this section only.

- What is the divinatory meaning of each card and how does Binah influence this meaning?

- As you go through the exercises, you can and should develop your own understanding and meaning of each card based on your insights. How does your understanding of Binah change your personal understanding of the cards?

- If you are doing the exercises for Binah for an entire month, consider doing one Tarot card each week.

BINAH—UNDERSTANDING (בינה)

Binah means "understanding" in Hebrew. It's the understanding one gets from action and experience. It's the experience of something that gives you the insight needed to develop wisdom.

- Think about what understanding means to you and how it relates to this Sephirah.

- How does understanding go with wisdom? Give examples of the necessity of developing understanding in order to have wisdom.

- Was there a time when you were trying to explain something to someone and they didn't understand because they did not have your experience?

- Think of an experience that changed how you understood something.

- Think of an experience that gave you understanding.

ADDITIONAL CORRESPONDENCES

Now that you have developed a better understanding of Binah, let's move beyond *777* to create your own correspondences. There are two senses not addressed by *777*. One is taste; the other is sound.

- Choose a food based on your understanding of Binah.

- Choose a song or type of music. You may select songs from different genres (classical, rock, etc.) and have multiple columns, like the god and goddess columns in the table in Appendix B.

- Continue this with other categories—occupations, drinks, movies, etc. Add these categories to your own *777* chart in Appendix B and use these same categories throughout the Sephiroth.

REVIEWING THE SUPERNAL TRIAD: THE UNION OF CHOKMAH AND BINAH

Pause now to consider the three Sephiroth you have just studied. They are called the Supernal Triad and they exist above the abyss. They are the hardest, in my opinion, to work with from a tactile perspective because they are the realm of inspiration (Briah) and spirituality (*Atziluth*)—neither of which is easily represented by physical items.

> Unity transcends consciousness. It is above all division. The Father of thought—the Word—is called Chaos—the dyad. The number Three, the Mother, is called Babalon. In connection with this the reader should study "The Temple of Solomon the King" in *Equinox* I, V, and *Liber 418*.
>
> This first triad is essentially unity, in a manner transcending reason. The comprehension of this Trinity is a matter of spiritual experience. All true gods are attributed to this Trinity.[14]

---

14 Crowley, *Magick*, p. 138.

Below the Abyss of Da'ath (which is not a Sephirah and should not be represented on your Tree as such), we are in the area of the intellect (*Yetzirah*) and eventually the physical world (*Assiah*).

> An immeasurable abyss divides it from all manifestations of Reason or the lower qualities of man. In the ultimate analysis of Reason, we find all reason identified with this abyss. Yet this abyss is the crown of the mind. Purely intellectual faculties all obtain here. This abyss has no number, for in it all is confusion.[15]

It is much easier to understand the Sephiroth from here on out with tactile and creative activities.

ADDITIONAL EXERCISES

- Get a larger table or altar and place all of the items from both the Binah and Chokmah altars on it. Specifically, combine the linga and yoni.

- Examine all of these items. How do they work together?

- Identify the items that cannot work or function without each other.

- Why are Chokmah and Binah never worked alone?

- When you are ready to move on to the next Sephirah, move the combined altar to an appropriate room in your house if you can. What room would you chose? Why?

---

15 Crowley, *Magick*, p. 138.

THE
SECOND
TRIAD

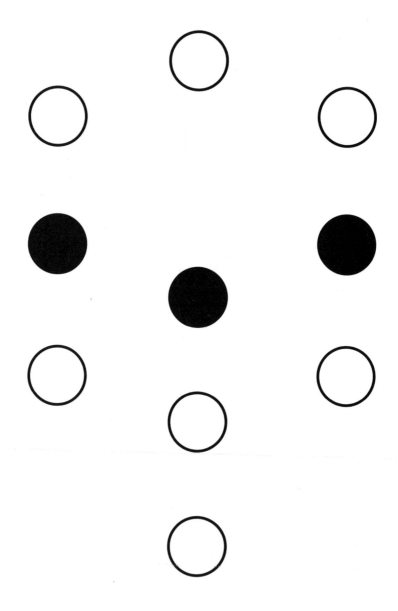

Figure 6. The Second Triad.

CHESED, GEVURAH, AND TIPHARETH make up the next triad on the Tree. They exist below the abyss and are in the middle of the Tree. Ending with Tiphareth, they contain the first knowable and tangible aspects of "God."

THE MAGICAL THEORY
OF THE UNIVERSE

Da'ath is the abyss that is between the Supernal Triad and the lower seven. It, in itself, is not a Sephirah, but rather a journey one must make from duality to unity.

The names of the lower Sephiroth come from I Chronicles 29:11, a passage familiar to anyone raised in either the Christian or Jewish traditions.

> Yours, Adonai, is the greatness, [Chesed] the power, [Gevurah] the glory, [Tiphareth] the victory [Netzach] and the majesty; [Hod] for everything [Yesod] in heaven and on earth is yours. The kingdom [Malkuth] is yours, Adonai; and you are exalted as head over all.

FIXED SIGNS

Gevurah represents the first of the Fixed signs of the zodiac. The Fixed signs are those in the middle. They are the middle of the seasons: the brightest days of spring, the hottest days of summer, the darkest nights of winter. They are the powerful and stable aspects of the zodiac—Taurus, Leo, Scorpio, and Aquarius. They are immovable.

The Fixed signs are represented by the Fives, Sixes, and Sevens of the Tarot. They are 31 degrees to 60 degrees of the zodiacal wheel (see table 3).

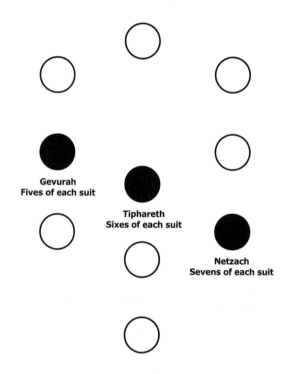

Figure 7. The fixed signs. Three Sephiroth associated with the Fixed Signs, Taurus, Leo, Scorpio, and Aquarius.

Table 3. The Fixed Signs and Their Associations

Fixed Signs						
Taurus	Earth	Disks	Heart of spring	31–40°	Five of Disks	Gevurah
				41–50°	Six of Disks	Tiphareth
				51–60°	Seven of Disks	Netzach
Leo	Fire	Wands	Heart of summer	31–40°	Five of Wands	Gevurah
				41–50°	Six of Wands	Tiphareth
				51–60°	Seven of Wands	Netzach
Scorpio	Water	Cups	Heart of fall	31–40°	Five of Cups	Gevurah
				41–50°	Six of Cups	Tiphareth
				51–60°	Seven of Cups	Netzach
Aquarius	Air	Swords	Heart of winter	31–40°	Five of Swords	Gevurah
				41–50°	Six of Swords	Tiphareth
				51–60°	Seven of Swords	Netzach

CHESED
COVENANT/MERCY
חסד

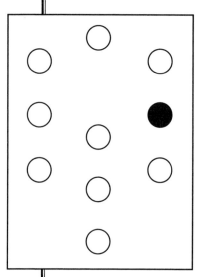

Color: Blue

Zodiacal and Planetary Representation: Sphere of Jupiter ♃

Tarot Cards: The 4 Fours—Completion (Wands), Luxury (Cups), Truce (Swords), Power (Disks)

Perfume: Cedar

Magical Weapons: Wand, Scepter, Crook

Precious Stones: Amethyst, Sapphire

God or Goddess Statues: Jupiter (Roman), Poseidon (Greek), Amoun (Egyptian)

Animal, Real or Imaginary: Unicorn

Plants, Real or Imaginary: Olive, Shamrock

Magical Power: Vision of Love

Additional Associations: Mercy, generosity, benevolence, Gedulah, covenants, laws, strict interpretation of the *logos*, action

The Sephirah of Chesed is the fourth emanation on the Tree of Life. The word *Chesed* has no direct translation and has been understood to mean "loving kindness" or "mercy." This is the home of the old, wise, benevolent king. It is the mercy the king acquires once he has received wisdom and understanding. It is the Sephirah of authority—the authority of the king and queen. It's the authority that comes with great leadership.

This is the Sephirah of true love—the love of a parent for a child, the deep love that comes with time and age. *Chesed* is sometimes translated into Greek as *agape*—love.

The word *Chesed* is also understood as a covenant or legal commitment. It is the covenant that a parent creates by making the decision to have a child, the covenant between a king and queen and their people. It's strict legal observation and commitment. Chesed is the king on the throne, the constitutional leader, the leader who makes the laws.

> Below the abyss we find the moral qualities of Man, of which there are six. The highest is symbolized by the number Four. Its nature is fatherly; Mercy and Authority are the attributes of its dignity . . .
>
> Each conception is, however, balanced in itself. Four is also Daleth, the letter of Venus; so that the mother-idea is included. Again, the Sephira of 4 is Chesed, referred to Water. 4 is ruled by Jupiter, Lord of the Lightning (Fire) yet ruler of Air. Each Sephira is complete in its way.[1]

ACQUIRE AND FURNISH YOUR ALTAR

Zodiacal and Planetary Representation and the Tarot Cards

- Research Jupiter.

- Place a representation of Jupiter on your altar.

- Place the 4 Fours of the Tarot on your altar—Completion (Wands), Luxury (Cups), Truce (Swords), Power (Disks)

---

1 Crowley, *Magick*, p. 138.

Perfume

For Chesed, the incense is cedar, chosen primarily for its protective nature.

Magical Weapons

For Chesed, the magical weapons are the wand, scepter, or crook. The magical weapons of Chesed are more symbolic than practical. They symbolize the will, power, and mercy of the magician. The wand is the symbol of the will of the magician. The scepter is a symbol of the power of the king or queen. The crook is the counter to the scourge of Gevurah and represents the mercy of the king.

Even though they apparently do not possess a utilitarian purpose, do not underestimate the use of these weapons as symbols of power and authority. The Queen of England possesses a scepter that is used in ceremonial functions, but not wielded daily. Catholic priests use a scepter during Holy Week—usually one with a sphere and a cross on top.

Osiris carried a crook and a flail. The crook represents the shepherd and the flail the farmer. These two unite under the king, who mediates between the two. The crook represents mercy—as the shepherd tends and cares for his flock, so does the king tend and care for his people.

> The Magick Wand is thus the principal weapon of the Magus; and the *name* of that Wand is the Magical Oath.
> The will being twofold is in Chokmah, who is the *logos*, the Word; hence some have said that the Word is the Will. Thoth the Lord of Magic is also the Lord of Speech; Hermes the messenger bears the Caduceus.[2]

- Now is the time, if you do not have one, to make your wand.

- You may also choose to procure or make a scepter and a crook.

Precious Stones

Amethyst and sapphire, both beautiful stones, can also be found in raw form; however, if you can procure a cut version of the gemstones, they are beautiful.

---

2 Crowley, *Magick,* p. 63.

- Why are amethyst and sapphire the stones of Chesed?

Clothing and Apparel

When purchasing or creating clothing for Chesed, regal materials of rich blue color fit for a king or queen are appropriate. A rich blue velvet cape lined with fur is very regal.

Animal, Real or Imaginary

The animal of Chesed is the unicorn, a controversial mythical creature. It shows up in many ancient histories, pictures, and stories, including biblical ones. Unicorns were believed to have existed until the nineteenth century. I point out, in this context, that it was believed that Sumeria was a fictional location until it was discovered in modern day Iraq in the late 1800s. Perhaps time and exploration will discover proof of unicorns as well. In the meantime, believe as you will.

- Research the myths of the unicorn. Why is this animal associated with Chesed?

- Are there any other animals that are not mythical that you would place in Chesed?

STUDY YOUR ALTAR

Once your Sephirotic altar is complete and ready for use, set aside time every day and perform the following exercises (at least once a day, but the more time you can spare the better). The time you choose is up to you.

- Light your incense. Close your eyes and breathe in the aroma. Let the scent take you to your altar.

- Study the Chesed altar intently.

- Move things around on the altar to facilitate other connections between items on the altar.

- Allow the word *Chesed* (Mercy) to repeat itself in your mind.

- Pick up the items on your altar and understand them. Remind yourself why each item is on the Chesed altar.

- If you chose a god or goddess to place on your altar, journal why this deity is appropriate to Chesed. What about the deity connects you to Chesed?

- Are there items on the altar that do not seem to be harmonious with each other?

- Look at each item and journal why you think each one is appropriate on the Chesed altar.

- Sometimes, the correspondences do not necessarily correlate to each other. Are there items on the altar that do not seem to relate to each other, even though they relate to Chesed?

CHESED, THE ZODIAC, AND THE TAROT[3]

- Jupiter is the planet of Chesed. What elements of Jupiter suggest Chesed? Journal.

- Chesed is the last of the Sephiroth represented by the Cardinal signs—Aries, Cancer, Libra, and Capricorn—and the last 10 degrees of each sign. How do the traits of a Cardinal sign find completion in Chesed?

- Study each of the Four cards individually, in the following order: Wands—Completion (Fire), Cups—Luxury (Water), Swords—Truce (Air), and Disks—Power (Earth).

---

3 Suggested additional reading, Lon Milo DuQuette, *Understanding Aleister Crowley's Thoth Tarot*, (York Beach, ME, Weiser Books, 2003), chapter 19, "The Small Cards," up to the description of each card individually, then read each section pertaining to the cards listed in this section only.

- Spend time contemplating each card and how it relates to Chesed.

- What is the divinatory meaning of each card and how does Chesed influence this meaning?

- As you go through the exercises, you can and should develop your own understanding and meaning of each card based on your insights. How does your understanding of Chesed change your personal understanding of the cards?

- If you are doing the exercises for Chesed for an entire month, consider doing one Tarot card each week.

CHESED—COVENANTS/MERCY (חסד)

Chesed implies "covenants" in Hebrew.

- Think about what covenants you have made in your life and what they mean to you and how they relate to this Sephirah.

- Why would covenants be appropriate in Chesed?

- When is mercy necessary?

- When does mercy represent weakness?

- How do wisdom and understanding (Chokmah and Binah) play a role in mercy?

- Was there a time when you were in a leadership role (as a manager, body master—any leadership role will do) when you had to make a tough decision and had to choose between showing mercy and being tough?

- How did your covenants help you make your decisions?

ADDITIONAL CORRESPONDENCES

Now that you have developed a better understanding of Chesed, let's move beyond *777* to create your own correspondences. There are two senses not addressed by *777*. One is taste; the other is sound.

- Choose a food based on your understanding of Chesed. What food would the Queen of England eat? What's royal food?

- Choose a song or type of music. You may select songs from different genres (classical, rock, etc.) and have multiple columns, like the *777* chart in Appendix B.

- Continue this with other categories—occupations, drinks, movies, etc. Add these categories to your own *777* chart in Appendix B and use these same categories throughout the Sephiroth.

GEVURAH—STRENGTH
גבורה

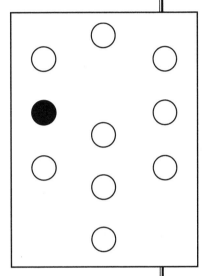

Color: Scarlet Red

Zodiacal and Planetary Representation: Sphere of Mars ♂

Tarot Cards: The 4 Fives—Strife (Wands), Disappointment (Cups), Defeat (Swords), Worry (Disks)

Perfume: Tobacco

Magical Weapons: Sword, Spear, Scourge, Chain

Precious Stone: Ruby

God or Goddess Statues: Mars (Roman), Ares (Greek), Horus (Egyptian)

Animal, Real or Imaginary: Basilisk

Plants, Real or Imaginary: Oak, Nux Vomica, Nettle

Magical Power: Vision of Power

Additional Associations: Power, Din, judgment, fear, severity, justice served, stringency, accountability, limitation, restriction, passion uncontrolled

The Sephirah of Gevurah is the fifth emanation on the Tree of Life. Gevurah means "strength" and "severity." The color associated with Gevurah is scarlet red, the red of blood. Of all the Sephiroth, Gevurah most easily becomes unbalanced. It was an out-of-balance Gevurah that caused the Qlippoth to come into being.[4] It was an out-of-balance Gevurah that caused Samael to manifest. Unbalanced power or strength has caused many of history's tragedies.

Gevurah is where God punishes failures and sins. It's the warrior God who imposes the penalties of the decisions of Chesed.

ACQUIRE AND FURNISH YOUR ALTAR

Zodiacal and Planetary Representation and the Tarot Cards

- Research Mars.

- Place a representation of Mars on your altar. Mars is the planet of Gevurah. Mars, the god of war, can be represented in a number of ways. Mars is the red planet, so a red sphere with the Mars glyph will work. The glyph in blood would be most appropriate (yours or an animal's, not someone else's!).

- Place the 4 Fives on your altar—Strife (Wands), Disappointment (Cups), Defeat (Swords), and Worry (Disks).

Perfume

Tobacco is a severe incense, so use it with caution. Combining it with a resin can make its use easier on you. Don't take up smoking. Crowley wasn't fond of this attribute, but understood tobacco's use as a male fighter primal bonding activity and appropriate to aspects of Gevurah (at the turn of the century at least).

---

4 The Qlippoth constitute the negative, or evil, Tree of Death.

- Think about old movies; how were men and women who smoked portrayed? Two suggestions are *Basic Instinct* or *Iwo Jima*.

- Think of other times when smoking is used for bonding. How about smoking as a sign of power or authority?

- If you smoke tobacco, how does it make you feel? Does it give you a sense of power or authority?

- Research the Native American "peace pipe." Is this a Gevurah practice?

- Now may be a good time for a trip to a cigar bar to share a cigar with a friend or someone with whom you want to bond. (You can add some cognac and have a toast to Crowley.)

A possible incense substitution for tobacco is dragon's blood, which is a Mars incense. Dragon's blood, when burned, bubbles like blood and the smell is strong and not particularly pleasing.

Magical Weapons

For Gevurah, the magical weapons are the sword, spear, scourge, and chain. These are all great weapons for any magician to have. If you don't have these already, acquire at least one of them for this working and work on acquiring the others.[5]

- As you acquire these weapons, use them, study them; understand how they differ both in utilitarian use and magical use. Journal!

SWORD

Acquiring your sword should take some thought. I have a number of swords for different workings, including one specifically for Gevurah workings. My Gevurah sword is a real sword, capable of battle. It's not a ceremonial sword. I wanted something that truly represented Mars, war,

---

5 Suggested additional reading, Aleister Crowley, *Magick*, Book IV, Part II, chapter IV, "The Scourge, the Dagger and the Chain" and chapter VIII, "The Sword."

and strength. I also have a dagger that I have consecrated to Gevurah. I keep it under my pillow for security.

- What kind of swords do you have?

- Are any of them appropriate for use with Gevurah?

> *Qabalah is fluid and alive. It is everything and nothing. Don't be afraid to let it grow and develop beyond the very limited scope of other perspectives and understandings. It is your universe and your perspective of how the universe works. Your understanding is going to be unique and correct.*

SPEAR

The term "spear" is sometimes analogous to the word "lance." The Spear of Destiny is also called the Lance of Longinus. For this reason, it is my opinion that the spear and lance can be used interchangeably.

This is a good time to read *Parzival* or to see the Wagner opera *Parsifal*. If you live in Europe, visit Neuschwanstein, a castle of Ludwig II, and see the Singing Room with the tapestries laying out the story of *Parsifal*. (I have been there; it's amazing!)

- Why does the spear or lance belong in Gevurah?

SCOURGE

A scourge is a whip or lash. Crowley tells us:

> The Scourge keeps the aspiration keen: the Dagger expresses the determination to sacrifice all; and the Chain restricts any wandering.[6]

The scourge has a long history. It has been used punitively by religious and secular groups.

- Study the historical use of the scourge.

---

6 Crowley, *Magick,* p. 58.

Crowley gives a description of the scourge in *Magick* (Book IV). This is a pretty severe scourge, but definitely would make its point.

> The Scourge should be made with a handle of iron; the lash is composed of nine strands of fine copper wire, in each of which are twisted small pieces of lead. Iron represents severity, copper love, and lead austerity.[7]

A number of initiatory systems have used the scourge as part of their initiations (A∴ A∴ and witchcraft, to name two).

- If you are an initiate of an organization that has used this as part of its initiation, examine its role with regard to Gevurah.

While the flail is not listed as a weapon of Gevurah, the fact that it balances the crook in the hands of Osiris makes it a good addition to the attributions of Gevurah. While we understand the flail as a weapon interchangeable with the scourge, in ancient times, it was actually an agricultural instrument. It was used by the ancient Egyptians to thresh wheat, while the crook was associated with herding sheep.

CHAIN

The chain Crowley describes has 333 links, the number of Choronzon, the completely unrestricted and undisciplined mind. Make your chain your own. How many links should your chain have to bind your wandering? To help you focus?

- Make a chain necklace of small links and wear it daily during this working.

Precious Stone

The ruby is a precious gem and cut versions of it are expensive. It is preferable to obtain a cut ruby, however, not a rough one. It can be a chip and doesn't have to be set in any jewelry. Borrow one if you have to, but get a real ruby, not a synthetic one.

---

7 Crowley, *Magick*, p. 59.

> *For all of the gemstones of the Sephiroth, you can purchase inexpensive faceted rondells on a string.*

Clothing and Apparel

Wearing a warrior's outfit is appropriate. I once did a Gevurah working where I asked all the attendants to come in a warrior's outfit of their choosing. I had everything from a Japanese warrior to someone in his U.S. military fatigues. I wore an Aztec warrior outfit.

A power suit or outfit that makes you feel strong, powerful, and confident is also appropriate dress for this work.

Animal, Real or Imaginary

The animal of Gevurah is the basilisk, an imaginary animal. European legends and myths are filled with stories of the basilisk. It's the king of killers, since it can kill with only a glance. There are a number of literary references to the basilisk.

- Research and journal why the basilisk is associated with Gevurah.

- Is there a real animal you would associate with Gevurah? Why?

Plants, Real or Imaginary

Plants associated with Gevurah are the oak, nux vomica, nettle, and hickory. If you use nettle, handle it with care; it's called stinging nettle for a reason. Nettle tea is supposed to control blood pressure, making it a good drink for a Gevurah working. *Please don't use nux vomica for your workings as an incense or tea, etc. It's a deciduous tree that contains strychnine.*

The mighty oak and the very hard hickory are great trees to use on your Gevurah altar. They also make great shafts for your spear or scourge.

- Go to the woods and learn to identify both oak and hickory. Put a leaf from each in your journal.

STUDY YOUR ALTAR

Once your Sephirotic altar is complete and ready for use, set aside time every day and perform the following exercises (at least once a day, but the more time you can spare the better). The time you choose is up to you.

- Light your incense.

- Close your eyes and breathe in the aroma. Let the scent take you to your altar.

- Study the Gevurah altar intently.

- Move things around on the altar to facilitate other connections between items on the altar.

- Allow the word *Gevurah* (Strength and Judgment) to repeat itself in your mind.

- Pick up the items on your altar and understand them. Remind yourself why each item is on the Gevurah altar.

- Make some nettle tea to drink when studying your altar.

- If you chose a god or goddess to place on your altar, journal why this deity is appropriate to Gevurah. What about the deity connects you to Gevurah?

- Look at each item and journal why you think each one is appropriate on the Gevurah altar.

- Sometimes, the correspondences do not necessarily correlate to each other. Are there items on the altar that do not seem to relate to each other, even though they relate to Gevurah?

GEVURAH, THE ZODIAC, AND THE TAROT[8]

- Mars is the planet of Gevurah. What elements of Mars suggest Gevurah? Journal.

- Gevurah is the first of the Sephiroth represented by the Fixed signs—Taurus, Leo, Scorpio, and Aquarius—and the degrees 31 through 40 of each sign. How do the traits of a Fixed sign manifest in Gevurah?

- Study each of the Five cards of the Tarot individually, in the following order: Wands—Completion (Fire), Cups—Luxury (Water), Swords—Truce (Air), and Disks—Power (Earth).

- Spend time contemplating each card and how it relates to Gevurah.

- What is the divinatory meaning of each card and how does Gevurah influence this meaning?

- As you go through the exercises, you can and should develop your own understanding and meaning of each card based on your insights. How does your understanding of Gevurah change your personal understanding of the cards?

- If you are doing the exercises for Gevurah for an entire month, consider doing one Tarot card each week.

GEVURAH—STRENGTH (גבורה)

Gevurah means "strength" in Hebrew. Think about what strength means to you and how it relates to this Sephirah.

---

8 Suggested additional reading, Lon Milo DuQuette, *Understanding Aleister Crowley's Thoth Tarot* (York Beach, ME: Weiser Books, 2003), chapter 19, "The Small Cards," up to the description of each card individually, then read each section pertaining to the cards listed in this section only.

- Think historically. Name leaders who have functioned in Gevurah to their detriment and others'.

- Look at your own leadership positions. Are they ever out-of-balance Gevurah? Do you wield power with strength, mercy, understanding, and wisdom?

- Were there times when your desire for power created an overbearing amount of strength, resulting in your own "Samael"?

WEAPONS OF WAR

The weapons of war look great lying on an altar, but you will appreciate them more if you learn how to use them. These exercises are about the utilitarian use of the weapons.

- Check out your local YMCA or fencing club and take a fencing class. It's expensive to get deeply into fencing, but you may be able to take an introductory class to see if you like it.

- Make a spear, then go off into the woods and learn how to use it. Set up a target and practice throwing the spear at the target. It's not as easy as it looks.

- The scourge is a little more challenging. If you have someone who will let you practice using the scourge, awesome! But you should also feel the pain of the scourge as well!

- Along these lines—in a safe environment, and only if someone will let you—bind them in chains. It's also a valuable experience to spend some time bound in chains yourself.

- How did learning the utilitarian use of these weapons assist you in understanding their magical use?

ADDITIONAL CORRESPONDENCES

Now that you have developed a better understanding of Gevurah, let's move beyond *777* to create your own correspondences. There are two senses not addressed by *777*. One is taste; the other is sound.

- Choose a food based on your understanding of Gevurah. Red meat is rich in iron and is associated with battle. If you eat red meat, have it cooked medium-rare to rare, so you can experience the blood of the animal that was sacrificed for your meal.

- Choose a song or type of music. You may select songs from different genres (classical, rock, etc.) and have multiple columns, like the god and goddess columns in the *777* chart in Appendix B.

- Continue this with other categories—occupations, drinks, movies, etc. Add these categories to your own *777* chart in Appendix B and use these same categories throughout the Sephiroth.

LEADERSHIP

Liber Librae sub figurâ XXX (The Book of Balance) explains the excesses of Gevurah and Chesed well:

> Remember that unbalanced force is evil; that unbalanced severity is but cruelty and oppression; but that also unbalanced mercy is but weakness which would allow and abet Evil.[9]

If Gevurah is out of balance, then the leadership becomes cruel and oppressive. There is a great wisdom in understanding when strength becomes cruelty. If Chesed is out of balance, then the leadership becomes weak and the king will be overthrown. Just as there is wisdom in understanding when strength becomes cruelty, there is equal wisdom in knowing when mercy becomes weakness. It's a common formula in stories—the

---

9 Crowley, *Magick*, p. 669.

old kindly king who wants to use diplomacy to solve a problem versus the hotheaded prince who wants to fight.

- If you are currently in a leadership position, now is a good time to evaluate your leadership style. Does it reflect more of Chesed or Gevurah?

- If you are not in a leadership position, select someone in your life who is and do the same evaluation.

- How about your political leaders? Do you perceive one party or group as more Gevurah in their ideology and another more Chesed?

- Which do you prefer and why?

- What could you or they do to be more balanced? Record your thoughts in your journal.

TIPHARETH—BEAUTY
תפארת

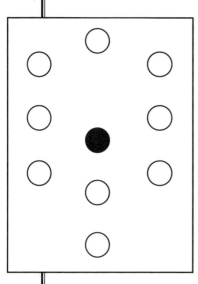

Color: Yellow

Zodiacal and Planetary Representation: Sphere of Sol ☉

Tarot Cards: The 4 Sixes—Victory (Wands), Pleasure (Cups), Science (Swords), Success (Disks)

Perfume: Olibanum

Magical Weapons: The Lamen or Rosy Cross

Precious Stones: Topaz, Yellow Diamond

God or Goddess Statues: Apollo (Roman), Apollo (Greek), Ra (Egyptian)

Animals, Real or Imaginary: Phoenix, Lion, Child

Plants, Real or Imaginary: Acacia, Bay, Laurel, Vine

Magical Powers: Vision of the Harmony of Things (also Mysteries of the Crucifixion)

Additional Associations: Beauty, balance, integrity, son, truth, harmony, milk and honey, The Holy One (blessed be he), bridegroom, prince

The Sephirah of Tiphareth is the sixth emanation on the Tree of Life. *Tiphareth* is the heart of the Tree. The word *Tiphareth* means "beauty." It is associated with balance, spirituality, compassion, and harmony. Every Sephirah has a Path connected to Tiphareth except Malkuth.

ACQUIRE AND FURNISH YOUR ALTAR

Color

Yellow is a color; gold is a metal. If yellow is referenced here, then it means the color yellow. If gold is referenced here, then it means a metal, not a color.

Zodiacal and Planetary Representation and the Tarot Cards

- Research the Sun.

- Place a representation of the Sun on your altar.

- Place the 4 Sixes on your altar—Victory (Wands), Pleasure (Cups), Science (Swords), and Success (Disks).

Perfume

For Tiphareth, the incense is olibanum, also known as frankincense.

- Research the history of frankincense.

- What are its historical uses?

- How does its historical use suggest Tiphareth?

Magical Weapons

For Tiphareth, the magical weapons are the Lamen and Rosy Cross. Technically, the Rosy Cross is considered a Lamen. In some traditions, it is to be worn over the heart.[10]

---

10 Suggested additional reading, Aleister Crowley, *Magick*, Book IV, Part II, "The Lamen."

The modern Lamen is, however, a simple plate which (being worn over the heart) symbolizes Tiphereth, and it should therefore be a harmony of all the other symbols in one. It connects naturally by its shape with the Circle and the Pentacle; but it is not sufficient to repeat the design of either.

The Lamen of the spirit whom one wishes to evoke is both placed in the Triangle and worn on the breast; but in this case, since that which we wish to evoke in nothing partial, but whole, we shall have but a single symbol to combine the two. The Great Work will then form the subject of the design.

In this Lamen the Magician must place the secret keys of his power.[11]

The Tarot cards of the Thoth Tarot have the Golden Dawn Rosy Cross on the reverse side.[12]

You can use the reverse side of the Tarot card on your altar, or you can make your own. A template is available as a download online. I have a sculpture of a Rose Cross hanging in my temple that I use as my magical weapon. I also have a tattoo of a Rose Cross over my heart.

- Begin to design your own personal Lamen. When you reach the chapter on Hod, you will study names and versicles and can incorporate those into your personal Lamen.

Precious Stones

Topaz is much easier to come by, but yellow diamonds are stunning. Since diamonds are the stone of Kether, yellow diamonds are a "less brilliant," but still stunning, reflection of Kether in Tiphareth.

Clothing and Apparel

Clothing for Tiphareth can be anything yellow. You can also get a patch made from the Lamen you design to stitch either to your altar or to an

---

11 Crowley, *Magick*, p.111.
12 Suggested reading, DuQuette, *Understanding Aleister Crowley's Thoth Tarot Deck,* where he gives a thorough explanation of the Rosy Cross that is on the back of the Thoth Tarot.

item of clothing you wear daily. A gold sunburst necklace is also something you can wear daily during your work.

STUDY YOUR ALTAR

Once your Sephirotic altar is complete and ready for use, set aside time every day and perform the following exercises (at least once a day, but the more time you can spare the better). The time you choose is up to you.

- Light your incense.

- Close your eyes and breathe in the aroma. Let the scent take you to your altar.

- Study the Tiphareth altar intently.

- Move things around on the altar to facilitate other connections between items on the altar.

- Allow the word *Tiphareth* (Beauty) to repeat itself in your mind.

- Pick up the items on your altar and understand them. Remind yourself why each item is on the Tiphareth altar.

- If you chose a god or goddess to place on your altar, journal why this deity is appropriate to Tiphareth. What about the deity connects you to Tiphareth?

- Look at each item and journal why you think each one is appropriate on the Tiphareth altar.

- Sometimes, the correspondences do not necessarily correlate to each other. Are there items on the altar that do not seem to relate to each other, even though they relate to Tiphareth?

TIPHARETH, THE ZODIAC, AND THE TAROT[13]

- The Sun is the planet of Tiphareth. What elements of the Sun suggest Tiphareth? Journal.

- Tiphareth is the second of the Sephiroth represented by Fixed signs—Taurus, Leo, Scorpio, and Aquarius—and the degrees 41 through 50 of each sign. Tiphareth is the heart of the Tree and the heart of the seasons in which it rules. It is the center of each of the four quadrants of the zodiac and the center of the Tree of Life. Tiphareth, perhaps more than any other of the Fixed signs, represents perfect balance, stability, and power.

- How do the traits of a Fixed sign manifest in Tiphareth?

- Study each of the Six cards of the Tarot individually, in the following order: Victory (Wands), Pleasure (Cups), Science (Swords), and Success (Disks).

- Spend time contemplating each card and how it relates to Tiphareth.

- What is the divinatory meaning of each card and how does Tiphareth influence this meaning?

- As you go through the exercises, you can and should develop your own understanding and meaning of each card based on your insights. How does your understanding of Tiphareth change your personal understanding of the cards?

- If you are doing the exercises for Tiphareth for an entire month, consider doing one Tarot card each week.

---

13 Suggested additional reading, DuQuette, *Understanding Aleister Crowley's Thoth Tarot*, chapter 19, "The Small Cards," up to the description of each card individually, then read each section pertaining to the cards listed in this section only.

This is a great time to begin doing Liber Resh (see the following ritual) as part of your daily routine.

- If you are already doing Liber Resh daily, spend the next month developing an understanding of it as a Tiphareth activity. Beyond the travels of the Sun, it is also about balance and harmony. Perform Resh at the specified times (sunrise, solar noon, sunset, and solar midnight) or at 6 a.m. and 6 p.m., and at noon and midnight.

. . . .the first essential is the dedication of all that one is and all that one has to the Great Work, without reservation of any sort. This must be kept constantly in mind: the way to do this is to practice Liber Resh.[14]

After at least a week of having aligned yourself daily with the Sun, journal about how things have changed. Consider your moods, your attitude toward others, and your thoughts throughout the day.

Liber Resh

Aleister Crowley wrote Resh as part of the A ∴ A ∴ Curriculum. Perhaps one of his best rituals, this seemingly simple rite contains within it meditation, magick, balance, and harmony, and is central to accomplishing the Great Work.

Let him greet the Sun at dawn, facing East, giving the sign of his grade. And let him say in a loud voice:

Hail unto Thee who art Ra in Thy rising, even unto Thee who art Ra in Thy strength, who travellest over the Heavens in Thy bark at the Uprising of the Sun. Tahuti standeth in His Splendor at the prow, and Ra-Hoor abideth at the helm. Hail unto Thee from the Abodes of Night!

Also at Noon, let him greet the Sun, facing South, giving the sign of his grade. And let him say in a loud voice:

---

14 Aleister Crowley, *Magick Without Tears* (Phoenix, AZ: Falcon Press, 1982), pp. 2–3.

Hail unto Thee who art Ahathoor in Thy triumphing, even unto Thee who art Ahathoor in Thy beauty, who travellest over the heavens in thy bark at the Mid-course of the Sun. Tahuti standeth in His Splendor at the prow, and Ra-Hoor abideth at the helm. Hail unto Thee from the Abodes of Morning!

Also, at Sunset, let him greet the Sun, facing West, giving the sign of his grade. And let him say in a loud voice:

Hail unto Thee who art Tum in Thy setting, even unto Thee who art Tum in Thy joy, who travellest over the Heavens in Thy bark at the Down-going of the Sun. Tahuti standeth in His Splendor at the prow, and Ra-Hoor abideth at the helm. Hail unto Thee from the Abodes of Day!

Lastly, at Midnight, let him greet the Sun, facing North, giving the sign of his grade, and let him say in a loud voice:

Hail unto thee who art Khephra in Thy hiding, even unto Thee who art Khephra in Thy silence, who travellest over the heavens in Thy bark at the Midnight Hour of the Sun. Tahuti standeth in His Splendor at the prow, and Ra-Hoor abideth at the helm. Hail unto Thee from the Abodes of Evening.

And after each of these invocations thou shalt give the sign of silence, and afterward thou shalt perform the adoration that is taught thee by thy Superior. And then do thou compose Thyself to holy meditation. Also it is better if in these adorations thou assume the God-form of Whom thou adorest, as if thou didst unite with Him in the adoration of That which is beyond Him.

Thus shalt thou ever be mindful of the Great Work which thou hast undertaken to perform, and thus shalt thou be strengthened to pursue it unto the attainment of the Stone of the Wise, the Summum Bonum, True Wisdom and Perfect Happiness.[15]

TIPHARETH—BEAUTY (תפארת)

Tiphareth means "beauty" in Hebrew. Think about what beauty means to you and how it relates to this Sephirah.

---

15 Crowley, *Magick*, p. 655–656.

- Study the meaning of the word "beauty."

- What do you consider beauty to be? Is it a physical, emotional, or character trait (to name a few possibilities)?

- What things in the world (not people) do you find beautiful? Why?

- Think of a beautiful place. If possible, go there.

- Reflect on why you find beauty there.

- What do you think, feel, see, and experience that exemplifies beauty?

TIPHARETH: A CAUTIONARY TALE

While the Sun is beautiful and gives us life and sustenance, it is also deadly. Read the story of Icarus. In his joy, he failed to see the danger of the Sun.

- What is the lesson of Icarus and the Sun?

ADDITIONAL CORRESPONDENCES

Now that you have developed a better understanding of Tiphareth, let's move beyond *777* to create your own correspondences. There are two senses not addressed by *777*. One is taste; the other is sound.

- Choose a food based on your understanding of Tiphareth.

- Choose a song or type of music. You may select songs from different genres (classical, rock, etc.) and have multiple columns, like the god and goddess columns in the *777* chart in Appendix B.

- Continue this with other categories—occupations, drinks, movies, etc. Add these categories to your own *777* chart in

Appendix B and use these same categories throughout the Sephiroth.

REVIEWING THE SECOND TRIAD

This is a good time to pause and consider the second triad you have just studied.

- How do these three Sephiroth complement and contradict each other?

- Did you notice that they are associated with three primary colors—blue, red, and yellow?

- How does Tiphareth provide balance to Gevurah and Chesed?

THE
THIRD
TRIAD

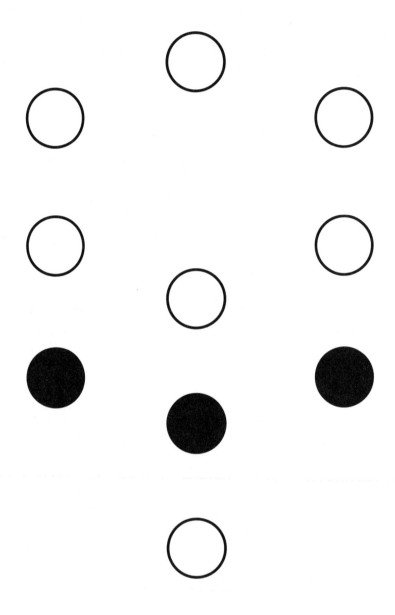

Figure 8. The Third Triad.

THE THIRD TRIAD CONSISTS of Netzach, Hod, and Yesod. These exist below a veil that runs beneath Tiphareth called the Veil of Paroketh. The Veil is just that—a veil. It is not a wall or impassable abyss; it is the illusion of these obstacles.

When you make your journey up the Tree from Malkuth and begin to work this universe you are creating, you will reach this Veil. Reaching Tiphareth, for many magicians, seems like an unattainable goal. It's the attainment of Knowledge and Conversation with your Holy Guardian Angel that seems to many to be impossible. It's not! It is the true beginning of your magical attainment—not its ultimate goal. The journey from the lower triad to the middle triad is blocked only by obstacles of your own choosing. You make the Veil whatever you set in your own way—fear, unworthiness, or a lack of opening yourself up to the beauty behind the Veil. Do not be afraid. Tear down your veils and see them as the illusions they are.

We have now moved into a realm that most of us understand and, to quote *The Wake World,* "many people stay here all their lives." It's the realm of our basest functions and behaviors. It's the realm of emotion, intellect, and sexuality, and of all our animal instincts. It's the easiest realm to understand and the hardest one to transcend.

MUTABLE SIGNS

The Mutable signs are well named. They represent the last four signs of each quadrant of the zodiacal wheel—Gemini, Virgo, Sagittarius, and Pisces. They are the transition of the seasons (see table 4). You know, those days when you start out in shorts and end up in a coat. Where each day is a surprise. They are that moment before the sunrise when light begins to show up in the sky, but the Sun has not reached the horizon. They are the moment when you know you made it through winter and that spring is around the corner. They can be both uplifting and frustrating.

Cardinal signs are explosive; Fixed signs are solid; Mutable signs are changeable. You never know what you are going to get with a Mutable sign. At the same time, they are adaptable and not stressed by change.

The last three Sephiroth—Hod, Yesod, and Malkuth—are represented by the Mutable signs. These Sephiroth are the farthest from their creation, from the will of the moment that created them. They are the least "pure" of the Sephiroth, particularly Malkuth.

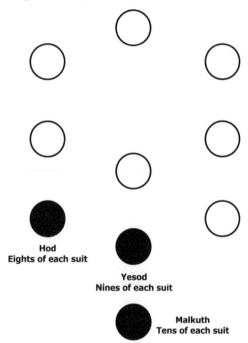

Figure 9. The Mutable signs. Sephiroth associated with the Mutable Signs, Gemini, Virgo, Sagittarius, and Pisces.

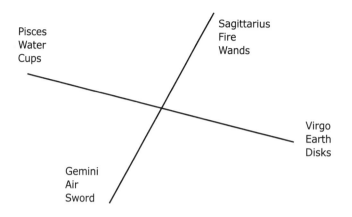

Pisces
Water
Cups

Sagittarius
Fire
Wands

Virgo
Earth
Disks

Gemini
Air
Sword

Table 4. The Mutable Signs and their Correspondences

Mutable Signs						
Gemini	Air	Swords	End of Spring	61–70°	Eight of Swords	Hod
				71–80°	Nine of Swords	Yesod
				81–90°	Ten of Swords	Malkuth
Virgo	Earth	Disks	End of Summer	61–70°	Eight of Disks	Hod
				71–80°	Nine of Disks	Yesod
				81–90°	Ten of Disks	Malkuth
Sagittarius	Fire	Wands	End of Fall	61–70°	Eight of Wands	Hod
				71–80°	Nine of Wands	Yesod
				81–90°	Ten of Wands	Malkuth
Pisces	Water	Cups	End of Winter	61–70°	Eight of Cups	Hod
				71–80°	Nine of Cups	Yesod
				81–90°	Ten of Cups	Malkuth

NETZACH—VICTORY
נצח

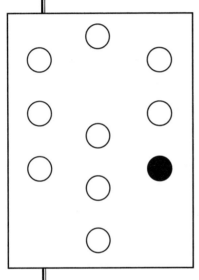

Color: Emerald

Zodiacal and Planetary Representation: Sphere of Venus ♀

Tarot Cards: The 4 Sevens—Valor (Wands), Debauchery (Cups), Futility (Swords), Failure (Disks)

Perfumes: Benzoin, Rose, Red Sandal

Magical Weapons: Lamp, Girdle

Precious Stone: Emerald

God or Goddess Statues: Venus (Roman), Aphrodite (Greek), Hathoor (Egyptian)

Animal, Real or Imaginary: Lynx

Plant, Real or Imaginary: Rose

Magical Power: Vision of Beauty Triumphant

Additional Associations: Emotion, kiss, creativity, unselfishness, clarity, lust, brightness, desire, devotion

The Sephirah of Netzach is the seventh emanation on the Tree of Life. *Netzach* means "victory." The victory of Netzach refers to the ability to persevere and to conquer using our passions and emotions to drive us forward. These do not have to be negative emotions. They can be joy and love, expressed through celebration, music, and dancing. It can be the pleasure of doing the ritual you wrote, playing the music you composed, painting the picture you studied.

ACQUIRE AND FURNISH YOUR ALTAR

Color

The color of Netzach is green. Green is a secondary color made up of the blue of Chesed, located just above Netzach, and the yellow of Tiphareth.

Zodiacal and Planetary Representation and the Tarot Cards

- Research Venus.

- Place a representation of Venus on your altar.

- Place the 4 Sevens on your altar—Valor (Wands), Debauchery (Cups), Futility (Swords), and Failure (Disks)

Perfumes

Benzoin, rose, and red sandal combined make a wonderful incense. Using a mortar and pestle, start out by grinding rose petals into a powder. Add benzoin resin and grind together. Finally, add a few drops of red sandalwood oil and grind all together. This is one of the best incenses I have ever made.

Magical Weapons

I have a beautiful antique oil lamp that I use as my magical lamp. With it, I use a variety of oil colors, depending on the ritual. Hint: If you can find oil in the primary colors, you can make any color by mixing them.

The lamp of Netzach is to be carried and represents the light of love that must be rekindled and kept lit.

- Get a lamp and make or purchase green oil for it. Alternatively, you can get a green lampshade or a green lightbulb—whatever makes your lamp green.

- Re-read the section on the lamp in *Magick* (Book IV) that is referenced in the chapter on Kether.

The girdle is a wonderful magical weapon with a long magical history. It was a symbol of strength for men and protection for women. It shows up in a number of mythological stories, including those of Hercules, Odysseus, the Amazons, and King Arthur. Perhaps the most famous girdle is Aphrodite's. Originally, it was used only for ornamentation; later, it came to be used to hold weapons (and much later to hold up pants and skirts).

ECCLESIA GNOSTICA CATHOLICA (E. G. C.) CLERGY

If you are a Priest or Priestess of the E. G. C., this is a good time to examine the line from the Gnostic Mass, "She bears the Sword from a red girdle," [1] *and the line from the* Book of the Law, *"Let the woman be girt with a sword before me."* [2]

- *How do you view these lines with your understanding of the girdle and Netzach?*

1 Crowley, *Magick*, p. 584.
2 Crowley, *Magick*, p. 314.

There is a lot of good information about the girdle and its later developments in mythology.

- Study the history of the girdle.

- Make a list as you go along of the various myths and meanings associated with the girdle. Then create your own girdle and record what your girdle is intended to do. Remember to wear it during your Netzach workings.

- What in the history of the girdle suggests a Netzach association?

Precious Stone

Emeralds, like rubies and diamonds, are precious gems and cut versions of them can be expensive. Again, it is preferable to obtain a cut emerald, not a rough one. It can be a chip and doesn't have to be set in any jewelry. Borrow one if you have to, but get a real emerald, not a synthetic one.

Clothing and Apparel

Consider something that evokes an emotion—a sentimental piece of jewelry or something you made or purchased because of an emotional connection. Don't forget your girdle.

STUDY YOUR ALTAR

Once your Sephirotic altar is complete and ready for use, set aside time every day and perform the following exercises (at least once a day, but the more time you can spare the better). The time you choose is up to you.

- Light your incense.

- Close your eyes and breathe in the aroma. Let the scent take you to your altar.

- Study the Netzach altar intently.

- Move things around on the altar to facilitate other connections between items on the altar.

- Allow the word *Netzach* (Victory) to repeat itself in your mind.

- Pick up the items on your altar and understand them. Remind yourself why each item is on the Netzach altar.

- Each day of this working, light your lamp, lift it, and think of someone you love and something nice you can do for them that day or the next. Then do it. Record this in your journal.

- If you chose a god or goddess to place on your altar, journal why this deity is appropriate to Netzach. What about the deity connects you to Netzach?

- Look at each item and journal why you think each one is appropriate on the Netzach altar.

- Sometimes, the correspondences do not necessarily correlate to each other. Are there items on the altar that do not seem to relate to each other, even though they relate to Netzach?

NETZACH, THE ZODIAC, AND THE TAROT[1]

- Venus is the planet of Netzach. What elements of Venus suggest Netzach? Journal.

- Netzach is the last of the Sephiroth represented by the Fixed signs—Taurus, Leo, Scorpio, and Aquarius—and the degrees 51 through 60 of each sign. Netzach is the depths of the seasons over which it rules. It is the depths of spring, summer, fall, and winter. It's that time when we are really tired of the current season and ready for the next one to begin. It is the time when we have morale issues—in winter, waiting for the Sun to return; in the heat of summer, waiting for some relief.

- How do the traits of a Fixed sign manifest in Netzach?

- Study each of the Seven cards of the Tarot individually, in the following order: Wands—Valor (Fire), Cups—Debauchery

---

1 Suggested additional reading, Lon Milo DuQuette, *Understanding Aleister Crowley's Thoth Tarot* (York Beach, ME: Weiser Books, 2003), chapter 19, "The Small Cards," up to the description of each card individually, then read each section pertaining to the cards listed in this section only.

(Water), Swords—Futility (Air), and Disks—Failure (Earth).

- Spend time contemplating each card and how it is related to Netzach.

- What is the divinatory meaning of each card and how does Netzach influence this meaning?

- As you go through the exercises, you can and should develop your own understanding and meaning of each card based on your insights. How does your understanding of Netzach change your personal understanding of the cards?

- If you are doing the exercises for Netzach for an entire month, consider doing one Tarot card each week.

NETZACH—VICTORY (נצח)

Netzach means "victory" in Hebrew. Think about what victory means to you and how it relates to this Sephirah.

As Netzach is the Sephirah of victory, consider wearing awards, medals, or other things you have earned. A martial arts belt works. This may seem like a Gevurah-type activity, and so it is. Netzach is directly opposite Gevurah through Tiphareth and shares a relationship.

- How does the victory and emotion of Netzach compare with the strength and power of Gevurah?

- Consider some creative activity you have completed. How did you feel when you completed the activity? Did you reward yourself?

- Creativity usually involves other people and their critique of your creation. How is this a Netzach function?

- Can you achieve victory if others condemn your creation?

- How do you define victory?

NETZACH AND EMOTIONS

Netzach is the seat of your emotions on a base level. This is the location of anger, jealousy, infatuation, joy, pleasure, happiness, and other such reactions. It's also where we get the drive to persevere and endure to conquer.

- Tap into your emotions. You may do any emotions you like, but I suggest that you do at least anger and happiness. You may do them in any order you like.

- For anger, be angry. Don't just think it; feel it. Get angry.

- Where do you feel it?

- How do you look when you are angry?

- How can you use this anger to be victorious, to persevere?

- For happiness, be happy. Feel it; don't just think it.

- What makes you happy?

- How does this help you persevere and accomplish your goals?

- Begin to understand how your emotions either block your achievements or contribute to their completion.

Just as you can spend a lifetime in Hod reading (you'll see soon enough), you can spend a lifetime in Netzach studying your emotions. Emotions are tools for us to use in the larger scheme of our work. Understanding what causes them and how they affect you enables you to use them effectively in your great work.

NETZACH AND VICTORY

Netzach is about doing, conquering.

- Have a Netzach party. Ask people to bring something they have created. It can be art, music, a poem—anything they created. Have people bring a food item that brings them joy.

Have music, belly dancing, drumming, etc. Set up a Venus altar. Ensure that everyone wears something green. (Isn't there a Western holiday that sounds very similar?) And have plenty of roses at your party. As I always say: Be creative with your party.

ADDITIONAL CORRESPONDENCES

Now that you have developed a better understanding of Netzach, let's move beyond *777* to create your own correspondences. There are two senses not addressed by *777*. One is taste; the other is sound.

- Choose a food based on your understanding of Netzach.

- In fact, many of us eat our emotions; we see food for its emotional function, joy!

- What food brings you joy?

- What food would you sell your soul to have? Chocolate? Sushi? What's your pleasure?

- If you have an eating disorder, Netzach may be the place to examine that issue. Food is number one for many in finding comfort or control. It can be pleasurable and joyous without being destructive and suppressing.

- Choose a song or type of music. You may select songs from different genres (classical, rock, etc.) and have multiple columns, like the god and goddess columns in the *777* chart in Appendix B.

- Continue this with other categories—occupations, drinks, movies, etc. Add these categories to your own *777* chart in Appendix B and use these same categories throughout the Sephiroth.

HOD—SPLENDOR
הוד

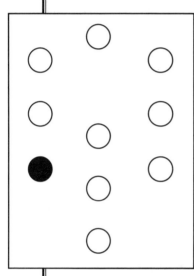

Color: Orange

Zodiacal and Planetary Representation: Sphere of Mercury ☿

Tarot Cards: The 4 Eights—Swiftness (Wands), Indolence (Cups), Interference (Swords), Prudence (Disks)

Perfume: Storax

Magical Weapons: Names and Versicles, Apron

Precious Stones: Opal, especially Fire Opal

God or Goddess Statues: Mercury (Roman), Hermes (Greek), Anubis (Egyptian)

Animals, Real or Imaginary: Hermaphrodite, Jackal

Plants, Real or Imaginary: Moly, Anhalonium Lewinii

Magical Power: Vision of Splendor

Additional Associations: Inspiration, transitory beauty, intellect, communication, trickster

The Sephirah of Hod is the eighth emanation on the Tree of Life. *Hod* means "splendor." Hod is where the magician dwells—usually too much. It's the home of the armchair magician—all theory and no practice. I liken Hod to theory and Netzach to practice. You need both to advance. You may have one hundred books on how to paint, but if you never lift the brush, the knowledge you've gained is illusory and only partially complete. It's the same with magick. You can read every book available, but if you never practice, you are not a magician by any stretch of the definition.

ACQUIRE AND FURNISH YOUR ALTAR

Color

Orange is a secondary color, derived from the red of Gevurah and the yellow of Tiphareth.

Zodiacal and Planetary Representation and the Tarot Cards

- Research Mercury.

- Place a representation of Mercury on your altar. There are a variety of ways to represent Mercury, including the element mercury, which is in a mercury thermometer. (Mercury is toxic; please do not break open a mercury thermometer.)

- Place the 4 Eights on your altar—Swiftness (Wands), Indolence (Cups), Interference (Swords), and Prudence (Disks).

Perfume

Storax is a resin, so it doesn't need to be mixed with anything because it will burn well. Crowley doesn't particularly like this association. In actual perfumery, storax is used as a fixative. It may be appropriate to use this as a base and add something to it, preferably a scent that stimulates communication or academic pursuits.

Magical Weapons

The "names" to which Crowley refers here are the names of God—the *logos*—probably in written form. There are a variety of ways to approach this magical weapon.

- For this Sephirah, I want you to establish your own divine name, your own magical name. If you have one, then use this time to develop a deeper understanding of the divinity of your magical name. If you do not have one, take one—at least for the duration of this working.

A versicle is "a short verse or sentence (as from a psalm) said or sung by a leader in public worship and followed by a response from the people . . . or a little verse."[2]

- I think this is a good moment to take a magical motto as well, a little "verse" that defines what you want to accomplish, either in general or with this working.

- Another option is to develop a mantra that you use when you meditate, walk, or perform other appropriate activities.

E. G. C. CLERGY

If you attend the Gnostic Mass, consider the collects:
- *Is there one you particularly like and would use as a meditation?*
- *How are the collects magical weapons?*
- *How are they associated with Hod?*

The apron here is, I believe, intended to be a Masonic-style apron. The design has an inverted triangle on the front of a square. I ordered a blank

---

2 *Merriam Webster Dictionary.*

apron from a Masonic supply house and have used it in a variety of rituals, including Goetic and Sephirotic workings. If you created your own Lamen during the Tiphareth working, you can put this on the front flap of your apron. You can also include some orange trim to remind you that the apron is the magical weapon of Hod. Aprons are also easy to make if you have a modicum of sewing skills.

Clothing and Apparel

Perhaps an orange headpiece, a hat, or a cover of some type will help remind you that Hod is the realm of intellect and communication.

Plants, Real or Imaginary

Moly is the herb given to Odysseus by Hermes to protect him from Circe; it is mythological. *Anhalonium lewinii* is an obsolete name for the peyote cactus that grows in the American Southwest and Mexico. Here we have a dilemma. One plant is mythical and the other illegal (in the United States). At this point, it becomes imperative to decide why these plants are associated with Hod and come up with a logical substitution. The previous exercises have given you the tools to study and come up with logical substitutions.

- What are the attributes of these plants that suggest Hod?

- What is a logical substitution for each or for both combined?

STUDY YOUR ALTAR

Once your Sephirotic altar is complete and ready for use, set aside time every day and perform the following exercises (at least once a day, but the more time you can spare the better). The time you choose is up to you.

- Light your incense.

- Close your eyes and breathe in the aroma. Let the scent take you to your altar.

- Study the Hod altar intently.

- Move things around on the altar to facilitate other connections between items on the altar.

- Allow the word *Hod* (Splendor) to repeat itself in your mind.

- Pick up the items on your altar and understand them. Remind yourself why each item is on the Hod altar.

- If you chose a god or goddess to place on your altar, journal why this deity is appropriate to Hod. What about the deity connects you to Hod?

- Look at each item and journal why you think each one is appropriate on the Hod altar.

- Sometimes, the correspondences do not necessarily correlate to each other. Are there items on the altar that do not seem to relate to each other, even though they relate to Hod?

HOD, THE ZODIAC, AND THE TAROT[3]

- Mercury is the planet of Hod. What elements of Mercury suggest Hod? Journal.

- Hod is the first of the Sephiroth represented by the Mutable signs—Gemini, Virgo, Sagittarius, and Pisces—and the degrees 61 through 70 of each sign. Hod is the first glimmer that the seasons are changing. It's that day you look outside and the snow is melting instead of piling up. It's the cool night of late summer reminding you that fall is near.

---

3   Suggested additional reading, Lon Milo DuQuette, *Understanding Aleister Crowley's Thoth Tarot* (York Beach, ME: Weiser Books, 2003), chapter 19, "The Small Cards," up to the description of each card individually, then read each section pertaining to the cards listed in this section only.

- How do the traits of a Mutable sign manifest in Hod?

- Study each of the Eight cards in the Tarot deck individually, in the following order: Wands—Swiftness (Fire), Cups—Indolence (Water), Swords—Interference (Air), and Disks—Prudence (Earth).

- Spend time contemplating each card and how it is related to Hod.

- What is the divinatory meaning of each card and how does Hod influence this meaning?

- As you go through the exercises, you can and should develop your own understanding and meaning of each card based on your insights. How does your understanding of Hod change your personal understanding of the cards?

- If you are doing the exercises for Hod for an entire month, consider doing one Tarot card each week.

HOD—SPLENDOR (הוד)

Hod means "splendor" in Hebrew. Dictionary.com defines splendor as:

1. brilliant or gorgeous appearance, coloring, etc.; magnifcence: *the splendor of the palace*

2. an instance or display of imposing pomp or grandeur: *the splendor of the coronation.*

3. grandeur; glory; brilliant distinction: *the splendor of ancient Greek architecture.*

4. great brightness; brilliant light or luster.

    - What is the most glorious or grand place you can think of?

    - What makes it glorious or grand?

- Think about what splendor means to you and how it relates to this Sephirah.

HOD AND THE INTELLECT

Hod is the seat of the intellect. Focus on things that improve your brain power. Just as an aside, "Hod" spelled backwards spells "Duh." Think about it.

- Listen to Mozart at least once a day for ten minutes.

- Play mental games—crossword puzzles, word games, anything that involves thinking—at least once per day.

- Memorize a chapter of the *Book of the Law* or another holy book.

HOD AND COMMUNICATIONS

Mercury is the messenger of the gods. We have become a "messenger" society through texting, instant messaging, and social networking.

- Every time you send a text message, think of Mercury and Hod. See this activity as a mercurial exercise. For many of us (yours truly included), that's a lot of focusing on Mercury!

- How does social networking change the way you communicate?

ADDITIONAL CORRESPONDENCES

Now that you have developed a better understanding of Hod, let's move beyond *777* to create your own correspondences. There are two senses not addressed by *777*. One is taste; the other is sound.

- Choose a food based on your understanding of Hod. "Brain food" is a good choice for foods corresponding to Hod—foods that contain Omega-3s and fiber. You can also add foods that contain antioxidants to your diet. It takes about three weeks for changes in your diet to improve your system, so stick with these changes through the Hod working and beyond if you can.

- Choose a song or type of music. You may select songs from different genres (classical, rock, etc.) and have multiple columns, like the god and goddess columns in the *777* chart in Appendix B.

- Continue this with other categories—occupations, drinks, movies, etc. Add these categories to your own *777* chart in Appendix B and use these same categories throughout the Sephiroth.

YESOD—FOUNDATION
יסוד

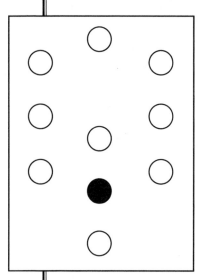

Color: Violet

Zodiacal and Planetary Representation: Sphere of Luna ☽

Tarot Cards: The 4 Nines—Strength (Wands), Happiness (Cups), Cruelty (Swords), Gain (Disks)

Perfumes: Jasmine, Ginseng, All Odoriferous Roots

Magical Weapons: Perfumes, Sandals, Altars

Precious Stone: Quartz

God or Goddess Statues: Diana (Roman), Diana of Ephesus (Greek), Shu (Egyptian)

Animal, Real or Imaginary: Elephant

Plants, Real or Imaginary: Banyan, Mandrake, Damiana

Magical Power: Vision of the Machinery of the Universe

Additional Associations: Astral, Moon, genitals of god, procreation, grounding, soul, well of souls, bridge, unconscious mind.

The Sephirah of Yesod is the ninth emanation on the Tree of Life. Yesod is an interesting Sephirah. *Yesod* means "foundation," suggesting it is the foundation of the Tree. Yet there is another Sephirah below Yesod called Malkuth. So why is Yesod the foundation instead of Malkuth? Malkuth is liminal. It is the connection between the lower and upper realms. Yesod is the first Sephirah that is truly only in the upper realm. By virtue of being solidly on the Tree of Life and not sullied by a direct connection to the lower realm, Yesod is the foundation on which the rest of the Tree relies.

ACQUIRE AND FURNISH YOUR ALTAR

Color

Violet correlates to the black of Malkuth and is the combination of the orange of Hod and the green of Netzach, or of the red of Gevurah and the blue of Chesed. Yesod is the balance between Netzach and Hod.

Zodiacal and Planetary Representation and the Tarot Cards

- Research the Moon.

- Place a representation of the Moon on your altar. There are a variety of ways to represent the Moon—for example, as a lunar glyph. There are lots of really good pictures of the Moon on the Internet that you can use, or you can take your own. You can also paint your own picture of the Moon. As always, be creative.

Note: Begin your Yesod working on the New Moon so you can observe the phases of the Moon throughout the month of your working.

- Place the 4 Nines on your altar—Strength (Wands), Happiness (Cups), Cruelty (Swords), and Gain (Disks).

Perfumes

Odoriferous roots are, by definition, those that have an odor. Examples are ginseng, ginger, galangal, and bamboo.

- Research some examples of odoriferous roots.

- Which ones are appropriate for Yesod?

Magical Weapons

Because perfume is the magical weapon of Yesod, be sure a casket of perfume is prominent on your altar. You will use perfume with most exercises in this book, but it is assigned as a magical weapon to Yesod. The perfume

rises up from the Earth to the heavens, to Yesod.[4]

Yesod is the realm of the astral plane. The sandals are the shoes with which you walk through the astral realm. Don't use them for anything but your Yesod working.

The altar of the magician is also a specific magical weapon for Yesod.

- Examine the altar you are using. Is it working for you? Use your altar only for magical work. This is a good time to dedicate your altar or altars for magical use.[5]

Figure 10. A censer.

This is also a good time to consider a permanent altar, if you do not have one—one that you will keep up and use for most of your magical workings. On your working magical altar, there should be only those things you need to do your current magical working, so that there are no distractions. If you are making a painting with only red paint but you have blue paint on your palette, you run the risk of having the blue contaminate the red and you may end up with purple and an entirely different working.

---

4 Suggested reading, Aleister Crowley, *Magick*, Book IV, Part II, chapter XVI, "The Magick Fire: with Considerations of the Thurible, the Charcoal, and the Incense."

5 Suggested reading, Crowley, *Magick*, Book IV, Part II, chapter III, "The Altar."

- What do you keep on your altar on a regular basis?

- Is your altar filled with items or do you have a clear altar?

Make sure your working space is devoted to its particular working.

Clothing and Apparel

Perhaps your sandals can be violet. If you get cloth sandals, they can be dyed violet.

Plants, Real or Imaginary

Crowley chooses these plants primarily due to their sexual nature. Yesod corresponds to the genitals of god in the Adam Kadmon view of the Tree as the idealized man.[6]

STUDY YOUR ALTAR

Once your Sephirotic altar is complete and ready for use, set aside time every day and perform the following exercises (at least once a day, but the more time you can spare the better). The time you choose is up to you.

- Light your incense.

- Close your eyes and breathe in the aroma. Let the scent take you to your altar.

- Study the Yesod altar intently.

- Move things around on the altar to facilitate other connections between items on the altar.

- Allow the word *Yesod* (Foundation) to repeat itself in your mind.

- Pick up the items on your altar and understand them. Remind yourself why each item is on the Yesod altar.

---

6 Adam Kadmon is the primordial man. He is used in Jewish and Gnostic texts to represent the first man.

- If you chose a god or goddess to place on your altar, journal why this deity is appropriate to Yesod. What about the deity connects you to Yesod?

- Look at each item and journal why you think each one is appropriate on the Yesod altar.

- Sometimes, the correspondences do not necessarily correlate to each other. Are there items on the altar that do not seem to relate to each other, even though they relate to Yesod?

- Record in your journal any emotions you have and the activities you do during the cycles to see if you notice any connection to the various stages of the Moon. You may need to do this over the course of a number of months to see if any patterns arise. Remember that the stages of the Moon move oceans. Since you are 55–60 percent water, they can have an effect on you as well.

YESOD, THE ZODIAC, AND THE TAROT[7]

- The Moon is the planet of Yesod. What elements of the Moon suggest Yesod? Journal.

- Yesod is the second of the Sephiroth represented by the Mutable signs—Gemini, Virgo, Sagittarius, and Pisces—and the degrees 71 through 80 of each sign. Yesod is the time when you don't really know what the season is. One week it's snowing; the next it's 75 degrees; then it's snowing again.

- How do the traits of a Mutable sign manifest in Yesod?

- Study the Tarot cards associated with Yesod, in the following order: Wands—Strength (Fire), Cups—Happiness (Water), Swords—Cruelty (Air), and Disks—Gain (Earth).

---

7 Suggested additional reading, Lon Milo DuQuette, *Understanding Aleister Crowley's Thoth Tarot* (York Beach, ME: Weiser Books, 2003), chapter 19, "The Small Cards," up to the description of each card individually, then read each section pertaining to the cards listed in this section only.

- Spend time contemplating each card and how it is related to Yesod.

- What is the divinatory meaning of each card and how does Yesod influence this meaning?

- As you go through the exercises, you can and should develop your own understanding and meaning of each card based on your insights. How does your understanding of Yesod change your personal understanding of the cards?

- If you are doing the exercises for Yesod for an entire month, consider doing one Tarot card each week.

YESOD—FOUNDATION (יסוד)

Yesod means "foundation" in Hebrew. Think about what foundation means to you and how it relates to this Sephirah.

- What do you consider your foundation or foundations?

- What happens if you lose your foundation?

- Consider putting a representation of your foundation on your Yesod altar.

YESOD AND THE ASTRAL

This exercise is important because it will serve as the foundation for the mystical tradition that is Qabalah.

If you have never experienced astral travel, now is a good time to start your astral work. I recommend following Crowley's instructions in *Liber O* for astral work.

> It may be added that this apparently complicated experiment is perfectly easy to perform. It is best to learn by "traveling" with a person already

experienced in the matter. Two or three experiments will suffice to render the student confident and even expert.[8]

- If you have already been doing astral work, add in the weapons of Yesod, burn incense, wear the sandals, and focus on Yesod as the astral plane.

- Record any differences in your journeys compared to those from before this working.

- How does Yesod, as the astral, become the foundation for Qabalistic workings?

YESOD AND THE MOON

- On the next Full Moon, take your altar outside (weather permitting) and study it under the light of the Full Moon. (If you can't go outside, find a suitable place where you can see the Moon—for instance, through a window.)

- Observe the Moon and how its light reflects on your altar.

- We know the Moon has an effect on us; it can move oceans after all. Can you feel or sense an effect from the Moon?

- Check the local news for crime rates, births, etc. during the Full Moon, New Moon, and the Half Moons. Is there a difference? Why?

ADDITIONAL CORRESPONDENCES

Now that you have developed a better understanding of Yesod, let's move beyond *777* to create your own correspondences. There are two senses not addressed by *777*. One is taste; the other is sound.

---

8   Crowley, *Magick*, p. 625.

- Choose a food based on your understanding of Yesod. What is a good lunar food?

- How about a foundational food item?

- The foundation is your anchor, the thing on which the rest of the process depends, so what is a foundational food?

- We usually build our meals around the entrée. What is a good lunar entrée?

- Why do you associate it with Yesod? Don't forget to journal your choice.

- Choose a song or type of music. You may select songs from different genres (classical, rock, etc.) and have multiple columns, like the god and goddess columns in the *777* chart in Appendix B.

- Continue this with other categories—occupations, drinks, movies, etc. Add these categories to your own *777* chart in Appendix B and use these same categories throughout the Sephiroth.

REVIEWING THE THIRD TRIAD

We have completed an examination of the final triad in the Tree of Life. Like Chesed and Gevurah above them, Netzach and Hod work together. The Zohar calls them the scales of balance. Hod is the inspiration; Netzach is the result of the inspiration. Hod is the play; Netzach is the performance. Hod and Netzach are the lovers; Yesod is the physical manifestation of this love.

- Consider an activity that involved both your intellectual abilities and your creative drive. Was there a difference in your perception of "victory" with the completion of this compared to a purely intellectual exercise? For example, reading a book versus writing one?

- This is a good time to delve into the creative process with follow through.

- Write a poem and publish it.

- Create a dance and perform it.

- Make an item of clothing and wear it.

Wherever your creative talents lie or wherever you find inspiration—create and then follow through! You may have ideas and inspiration for the greatest novel, but if you don't write it, you are stuck in Hod forever, thinking about how you *could* write a great novel.

MALKUTH,
THE
GATEWAY

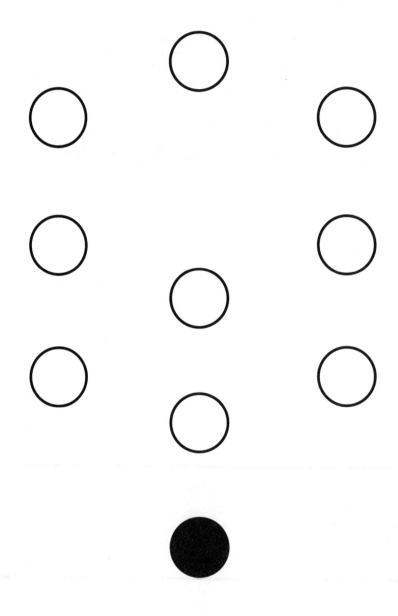

Figure 11. Malkuth.

MALKUTH IS THE GATEWAY SEPHIRAH. It is through Malkuth that we access the world of Qabalah. Malkuth is where all the aspects, energy, and attributions of the Tree flow into the material world. Malkuth, also called *Shekinah*, is feminine. She has no life of her own, but rather reflects all that is above and all that is below. She is the most vulnerable to corruption from below and from overactive Sephiroth above her.

Once you have completed this workbook and created your universe, Malkuth is where you will begin your magical journey back up the Tree. Malkuth, Tiphareth, and Kether all interact as the center of balance. Malkuth is where you must build a matrix of all the elements upon which you will do your Great Work up the Tree on your journey to Tiphareth and beyond.

Malkuth is Earth. She is pregnant with all possibility. From Malkuth you can go anywhere and do anything in your Qabalistic universe.

MALKUTH—KINGDOM
מלכות

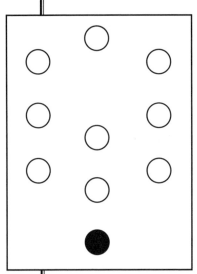

Colors: Citrine, Olive, Russet, Black

Zodiacal and Planetary Representation: Sphere of the Elements (The Earth) ⊕

Tarot Cards: The 4 Tens—Oppression (Wands), Satiety (Cups), Ruin (Swords), Wealth (Disks)

Perfume: Dittany of Crete

Magical Weapons: Magical Circle, Triangle

Precious Stone: Rock Crystal

God or Goddess Statues: Ceres (Roman), Persephone (Greek), Seb (Egyptian)

Animal, Real or Imaginary: Sphinx

Plants, Real or Imaginary: Willow, Lily, Ivy

Magical Powers: Vision of the Holy Guardian Angel or of Adonai

Additional Associations: Rose, well, fountain, Shekinah, daughter, princess, bride, sea, visible presence of God, burning bush.

The Sephirah of Malkuth is the tenth emanation on the Tree of Life. *Malkuth* means "kingdom." Malkuth is the most complex of all the Sephiroth. Representing all of the elements, it is the natural funnel for all of the other Sephiroth into the material plane. Malkuth has no nature of its own; even its color correspondences suggest a dulled version of the brilliant colors above it. It is entirely dependent on the energy above and below. Malkuth is the gateway into the world of the divine. It is one of two feminine Sephiroth on the Tree. It is also called the Shekinah.

ACQUIRE AND FURNISH YOUR ALTAR

Colors

These four colors are derived from less vibrant versions of the four Sephiroth above Malkuth. Citrine is a dull yellow (Tiphareth); olive is a dull green (Netzach); russet is a dull orange (Hod); black is the total darkening of violet (Yesod) and contains all colors. Malkuth is where the vibrancy of the divine light finally diminishes into the material plane.

Zodiacal and Planetary Representation and the Tarot Cards

- Place a representation of the Earth on your altar. Earth is probably the easiest of the planets to represent. Simply place a bowl full of dirt on your altar. You may also place a globe, or anything that reminds you of the Earth.

- Place the 4 Tens on your altar—Oppression (Wands), Satiety (Cups), Ruin (Swords), and Wealth (Disks).

Perfume

Dittany of Crete is an herb. It comes from Greece and has a variety of uses. Magically, it is believed that burning dittany of Crete causes spirits to manifest in the smoke. Malkuth is all about manifestation.

Magical Weapons

The circle is the realm of the magician. There are a variety of ways to create your magical circle. For the purposes of this exercise, the circle should be a physical circle. You may create the one described by Crowley in *Magick* (Book IV):

> **The Temple** represents the external Universe. The Magician must take it as he finds it, so that it is of no particular shape; yet we find written, Liber VII, vi, 2: "We made us a Temple of stones in the shape of the Universe, even as thou didst wear openly and I concealed." This shape is the Vesica Piscis; but it is only the greatest of the Magicians who can thus fashion the Temple. There may, however, be some choice of rooms; this refers to the power of the Magician to reincarnate in a suitable body.[1]
>
> **The Circle** announces the Nature of the Great Work.
>
> Though the Magician has been limited in his choice of room, he is more or less able to choose what part of the room he will work in. He will consider convenience and possibility. His circle should not be too small and cramp his movements; it should not be so large that he has long distances to traverse. Once the circle is made and consecrated, the Magician must not leave it, or even lean outside, lest he be destroyed by the hostile forces that are without.
>
> He chooses a circle rather than any other lineal figure for many reasons; e.g.,
>
> 1. He affirms thereby his identity with the infinite.
>
> 2. He affirms the equal balance of his working; since all points on the circumference are equidistant from the centre.
>
> 3. He affirms the limitation implied by his devotion to the Great Work. He no longer wanders about aimlessly in the world.[2]

For my circle, I cut a carpet remnant into a circle and then put the names of the Thelemic deities around the edge using glow-in-the-dark fabric paint.

---

1 Aleister Crowley, *Magick* (York Beach, ME: Weiser Books, 1998), p. 49.
2 Crowley, *Magick*, p. 51.

The triangle is used for the evocation of spirits. Each Sephirah has associated with it various entities. Those entities are associated with the four worlds. In order to evoke these entities, one needs a magical triangle. In Appendix A of this workbook is a chart of the spirits of the Sephiroth. Make your magical triangle so that you can use it to evoke these spirits.

There is a description of a magical triangle in the *Goetia*. This is the one most often used by magicians for evocation.

> It [the triangle] is to be made at two feet distance from the Magical Circle and it is three feet across. Note that this triangle is to be placed toward that quarter whereunto the Spirit belongeth. And the base of the triangle is to be nearest unto the Circle, the apex pointing in the direction of the quarter of the Spirit. . . . (Colours.—Triangle outlined in black; name of Michael black on white ground; the three Names without the triangle written in red; circle in centre entirely filled in in dark green.)[3]

However, there are other options and you can design your own (see figure 12).

Figure 12. The Goetic Triangle.

Precious Stone

Rock crystal is the precious stone corresponding to Malkuth. It is a colorless variety of quartz. *777* emphasizes the connection between Malkuth and Kether, so it's important that the quartz be colorless. A logical substitution here would be the man-made diamond, the cubic zirconia, since the diamond is the stone of Kether.

---

3 Aleister Crowley, *The Goetia* (San Francisco: Weiser Books, 2011), pp. 71–72.

Animal, Real or Imaginary

The sphinx is a mythological animal whose job it was to guard—for example, keeping unworthy people from entering the temple. The sphinx is a guardian here as well—the guardian of the gateway to the Sephirotic world through Malkuth. The sphinx can also be your guardian, protecting your temple from the profane.

Crowley discusses the symbolism of the sphinx in *Liber Aleph:*

> It is thus a Glyph of the Satisfaction and Perfection of the Will and of the Work, the completion of the True Man as the Reconciler of the Highest with the Lowest, so for our Convenience conventionally to distinguish them. This then is the Adept, who doth Will with solid Energy as the Bull, doth Dare with fierce Courage as the Lion, doth Know with swift Intelligence as the Man, and doth keep Silence with soaring Subtlety as the Eagle or Dragon. Moreover, this Sphinx is an Eidolon of the Law, for the Bull is Life, the Lion is Light, the Man is Liberty, the Serpent Love. Now then his Sphinx, being perfect in true Balance, yet taketh the Aspect of the Feminine Principle that so She may be partner of the Pyramid, that is the Phallus, pure Image of Our Father the Sun, the Unity Creative.[4]

In mythology, the sphinx challenged people with riddles.

- Set your sphinx up with information that only the worthy will know.

- Create a riddle, a password (a versicle, if you wish) and use it when you enter the world of the Sephiroth.

Plants, Real or Imaginary

- Take the earth from your altar and plant seeds of the plants of Malkuth in a pot.

- Reflect on this power of creation, of manifestation. You will be taking the seed, providing it with food, water, air, and sun-

---

4 Aleister Crowley, *Liber Aleph* (York Beach, ME: Samuel Weiser, 1991), p. 152.

light, and from this, manifesting a plant.

- Grow your own ivy or lily. Or, if you are really ambitious, plant a willow tree.

STUDY YOUR ALTAR

Once your Sephirotic altar is complete and ready for use, set aside time every day and perform the following exercises (at least once a day, but the more time you can spare the better). The time you choose is up to you.

- Light your incense.

- Close your eyes and breathe in the aroma. Let the scent take you to your altar.

- Study the Malkuth altar intently.

- Move things around on the altar to facilitate other connections between items.

- Allow the word *Malkuth* (Kingdom) to repeat itself in your mind.

- Pick up the items on your altar and understand them. Remind yourself why each item is on the Malkuth altar.

- If you chose a god or goddess to place on your altar, journal why this deity is appropriate to Malkuth. What about the deity connects you to Malkuth?

- Look at each item and journal why you think each one is appropriate on the Malkuth altar.

- Sometimes, the correspondences do not necessarily correlate to each other. Are there items on the altar that do not seem to relate to each other, even though they relate to Malkuth?

MALKUTH, THE ZODIAC,
AND THE TAROT[5]

- The Earth is the planet of Malkuth. What elements of the Earth suggest Malkuth? Journal.

- Malkuth is the last of the Sephiroth represented by the Mutable signs—Gemini, Virgo, Sagittarius, and Pisces—and the degrees 81 through 90 of each sign. It's the final transition into the next season.

- How do the traits of a Mutable sign manifest in Malkuth?

- Study each of the Tarot's Ten cards individually, in the following order: Wands—Oppression (Fire), Cups—Satiety (Water), Swords—Ruin (Air), and Disks—Wealth (Earth).

- Spend time contemplating each card and how it is related to Malkuth.

- What is the divinatory meaning of each card and how does Malkuth influence this meaning?

- As you go through the exercises, you can and should develop your own understanding and meaning of each card based on your insights. How does your understanding of Malkuth change your personal understanding of the cards?

- If you are doing the exercises for Malkuth for an entire month, consider doing one Tarot card each week.

MALKUTH—KINGDOM (מלכות)

Malkuth means "kingdom" in Hebrew. Think about what kingdom means to you and how it relates to this Sephirah. The definition of kingdom as provided by Dictionary.com is interesting as it relates to Malkuth.

---

5 Suggested additional reading, Lon Milo DuQuette, *Understanding Aleister Crowley's Thoth Tarot* (York Beach, ME: Weiser Books, 2003), chapter 19, "The Small Cards," up to the description of each card individually, then read each section pertaining to the cards listed in this section only.

1. a state or government having a king or queen as its head.

2. anything conceived as constituting a realm or sphere of independent action or control: *the kingdom of thought.*

3. a realm or province of nature, especially one of the three broad divisions of natural objects: *the animal, vegetable, and mineral kingdoms.*

4. biology—a taxonomic category of the highest rank, grouping together all forms of life having certain fundamental characteristics in common.

5. the spiritual sovereignty of God or Christ.

- How does each of these definitions relate to Malkuth?

- Do specific definitions relate more to your understanding of Malkuth? Why?

ADDITIONAL CORRESPONDENCES

Now that you have developed a better understanding of Malkuth, let's move beyond *777* to create your own correspondences. There are two senses not addressed by *777*. One is taste; the other is sound.

- Choose a food based on your understanding of Malkuth. I bake bread.

- Malkuth equals kingdom. What is a good food to serve to a king's court? A rich food, that is still earthy in nature?

- For your choice, why do you associate it with Malkuth? Don't forget to journal your choice.

- Choose a song or type of music. You may select songs from different genres (classical, rock, etc.) and have multiple columns, like the god and goddess columns in the *777* chart in Appendix B.

- Continue this with other categories—occupations, drinks, movies, etc. Add these categories to your own *777* chart in Appendix B and use these same categories throughout the Sephiroth.

CONCLUSION

ow that you have completed your study of the basics of the Tree of Life, it's time to work. It is my understanding that we move freely around the lower seven Sephiroth most of the time. Malkuth is the gateway to your upper world, whether you perceive that as another realm, a different dimension, or your own higher self.

We learned the Tree of Life by creating it. Now that it's grown, we can climb it and get other insights. Start at the bottom with Malkuth. Always begin and end formal workings in Malkuth; enter and exit through the gate. Next, establish your foundation in Yesod. Then study theory (Hod) and practice (Netzach).

You will begin to understand where you are at any given moment in your Qabalistic universe. It's not a single journey up the Tree. In fact, the Tree is an illusion—a convenient tool for our understanding and classification. In reality, you are in all the Sephiroth at the same time—they are endless. They are you. For example, if you are on an intellectual pursuit, that doesn't mean the rest of who you are is silent or nonexistent.

One of the versions of the Tree is the Onion (see figure 13). I think it helps to understand how all aspects of the Sephiroth are interconnected.

The Adam Kadmon version of the idealized human is another way to understand the Qabalah. Each Sephirah represents a different body part—hands, feet, genitals, heart—yet all one body, mind, and soul.

Remember that we worked only in the lower two worlds of Assiah, the material plane, and Yetzirah, the intellectual plane. As you repeat these

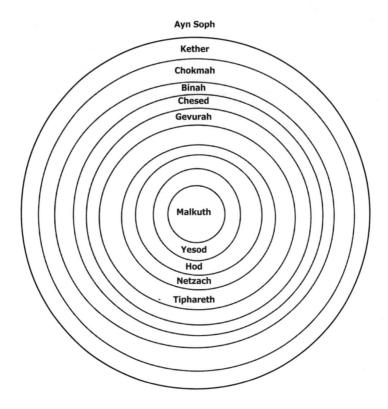

Figure 13. The Tree as the Onion.

exercises and develop a deeper understanding of the Sephiroth, your experiences will expand. Your ability to read theory and understand what is being said will also improve. This is not meant to be a one-time journey; it is meant to be a lifelong exploration.

It's time to continue your Qabalistic journey through the Sephiroth by way of the Paths of Wisdom. You have studied the first ten Paths in the Sephiroth. Your next step is to study the last twenty-two Paths, the roads or byways that connect the Sephiroth.

Appendix A:
Additional Exercises

ASTRAL MEDITATION

This exercise assumes some knowledge of meditation and astral work.

Before I do a working, I journey on the astral plane to the Sephirah in which I am working. To do this, I create my astral Qabalistic world.

I always begin and end in Malkuth.

- Journey to each Sephirah. Set each one up. How does each one look and feel?

- Are there other entities there?

- What items, colors, sounds, or locations do you perceive? For example, does Gevurah look like a big battlefield and Chesed a throne room?

- Set up gates with passwords and signs for entry—anything you think you need to see, feel, hear, taste, or smell in your Qabalistic universe.

- Once you are solidly in your Qabalistic universe, begin your working in the chosen Sephirah.

UNDERSTANDING THE TREE OF LIFE

The Sephiroth are in three columns (see figures 14, 15, and 16). These are called the Pillar of Mercy (Chokmah, Chesed, and Netzach), the Pillar of Severity (Binah, Gevurah, and Hod), and the center pillar, which has been referred to as the Pillar of Balance (Kether, Tiphareth, Yesod, and Malkuth).

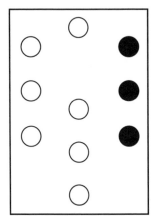
Figure 14.
The Pillar of Mercy.

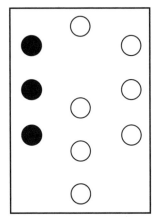
Figure 15.
The Pillar of Severity.

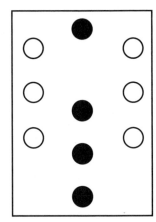
Figure 16.
The Pillar of Balance.

- Examine the three pillars.

- What about their attributions and your understanding of the Sephiroth contributes to this understanding?

- You may consider examining the altars of the three pillars separately.

- What connections to mercy, severity, or balance do you see in these correspondences?

TEN

The *Sefer Yetzirah* makes reference to the fingers. If you move Kether and Tiphareth to the right hand and Yesod and Malkuth to the left, you have all ten Sephiroth assigned to a hand. The understanding then becomes a tension between the two hands. It represents the spiritual tension of duality, while the joining of hands in prayer becomes the union (see figure 17).

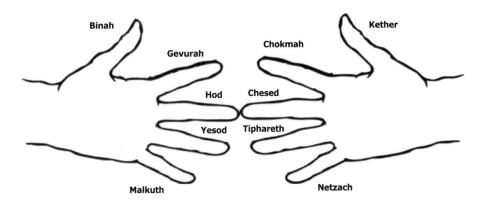

Figure 17. The attributions of the hands.

The left hand becomes the hand of strength; the right becomes the hand of love.

- Consider how the Sephiroth on the two hands reflect this assignment.

- Fold your hands in prayer, then look at the intersections and connections with the Sephiroth. Reflect and journal.

INVOKING THE SPIRITS OF THE SEPHIROTH

Since this workbook deals with the worlds of Assiah and Yetzirah, start with these entities using table 5 to identify the appropriate spirits.

Write an invocation or evocation ritual bringing the spirits to you, one Sephirah at a time. This can be done as an introduction to the spirit or as a request or command that each occupy its Sephirah in your Tree. Or you can have some other intent or purpose to your work, as ye will.

As your Qabalistic knowledge, wisdom, and understanding grow, so too will your ability to tap into the higher beings of each Sephirah.

Table 5. Invocation of Entities Associated with the Sephiroth

	Divine Name Atziluth	Archangels Briah	Choirs of Angels Yetzirah
Kether	AHIH (Ehieh)	Metatron	Chayoth ha-Qedesh or Holy Living Creatures
Chokmah	YH (Yah)	Ratziel	Auphanim or Wheels
Binah	YHVH ALHIM (Tetragrammaton Elohim)	Tzaphkiel	Aralim or Thrones
Chesed	AL (El)	Tzadkiel	Chashmalim or Lucid ones
Gevurah	ALHIM GBVR (Elohim Gibor)	Kamael	Seraphim or Fiery Ones
Tiphareth	YHVH ALVH VDAaTh (Tetragrammaton Eloah va-Da'ath)	Raphael	Melekim or Kings
Netzach	YHVH TzBAVTh (Tetragrammaton Tzabaoth)	Haniel	Elohim or Gods or Goddesses
Hod	ALHIM TzBAVTh (Elohim Tzabaoth)	Mikael	Beni Elohim or Sons of Gods or Goddesses
Yesod	ShDI AL ChI (Shaddai El Chai)	Gabriel	Kerubim or Strong Ones
Malkuth	ADNI MLK (Adonai Melek)	Sandalphon (Metatron)	Ashim or Virile Ones

MAGICAL POWERS—
THE JOURNEY TOWARD KNOWLEDGE
AND CONVERSATION

Study the magical powers associated with each Sephirah. While these are labeled magical powers, I associate them with mystical experiences. This journey is specifically the journey to your Holy Guardian Angel, your great work. The experience of the magical power of a Sephirah is intense and amazing. Keep working on it.

THE TAROT, THE ZODIAC,
AND THE TREE

As we discussed, each card in the Minor Arcana represents a Sephirah. The Aces are Kether. It gets interesting with Chokmah on down. The Twos, Threes, and Fours of the Minor Arcana represent the Cardinal signs of the zodiac—Aries, Cancer, Libra, and Capricorn. Cardinal signs are dominant. They are explosive. They usher in the seasons—spring, summer, fall, and winter, respectively. The Cardinal Sephiroth then become Chokmah, Binah, and Chesed.

The Fives, Sixes, and Sevens correspond to the Fixed signs of the zodiac—Taurus, Leo, Scorpio, and Aquarius. The Fixed signs are just that—fixed. They are stubborn and inflexible. They are the strength of the zodiac. They don't move or change much. These are the heart of the seasons. These are Gevurah, Tiphareth, and Netzach.

The Eights, Nines, and Tens are the Mutable signs of the zodiac—Gemini, Virgo, Sagittarius, and Pisces. These signs come at the end of the seasons—that time when the weather can go either way. Is it spring or summer? You know this time—the time when you're wearing shorts in the morning and a coat at night. These are the signs of change and transformation. They are Hod, Yesod, and Malkuth.

- Lay out the cards in the zodiac starting with Aries and the Two, Three, and Four of Wands. Taurus is the Five, Six, and Seven of Disks. Gemini is the Eight, Nine, and Ten of Swords.

- Then start with the Two, Three, and Four of Cups for Cancer, the Five, Six, and Seven of Wands for Leo, and the Eight, Nine, and Ten of Disks for Virgo.

- Next, lay out the Two, Three, and Four of Swords for Libra, the Five, Six, and Seven of Cups for Scorpio, and the Eight, Nine, and Ten of Wands for Sagittarius.

- Finally, lay out the Two, Three, and Four of Disks for Capricorn, the Five, Six, and Seven of Swords for Aquarius, and the Eight, Nine, and Ten of Cups for Pisces.

The cards are in the following order: Wands, Disks, Swords, and Cups, then Fire, Earth, Air, and Water, around the circle. This gives you a visual image of the universe using the Tarot. All thirty-six Decans of astrology, or the 360-degree circle, are represented, with each card being 10 degrees.

I have taught this exercise over the years to groups using someone's natal chart. I have also used this exercise to create my own magical circle using my own natal chart to position the cards in the formation they were in at the time of my birth.[1]

RITUALS—FINALLY!

Begin to write your own rituals utilizing your knowledge of Qabalah. This may already have happened organically. As your understanding of Qabalah grows, your worlds unite and there is no difference between the Qabalistic universe and your own. As above, so below.

---

1   For additional reading on this subject, read Lon Milo DuQuette, *The Chicken Qabalah*, chapter 9, "Chicken Tarot."

APPENDIX B

777 CHART

On pages 158–159 are excerpts of columns from *777*. These are the primary correspondences referenced in this workbook and are here for your convenience. There are additional columns in the actual book. Remember these are a starting point only and do not contain all possible correspondences even in the categories labeled. This is why I have included a blank table, on pages 160–161. Start your own columns, create your own connections, and make each Sephirah your own.

Since "Food" is one of the exercises in each chapter, I have started that one for you. Be creative and have fun.

I	II	II	III	VI	XIV	XLII
Sephiroth	Spelled out in English	Spelled out in Hebrew	Meaning	Alchemical/ Zodiacal	Tarot	Perfume
1	KETHER	כתר	CROWN	Sphere of the Primum Mobile (represented by Pluto)	The 4 Aces	Ambergris
2	CHOKMAH	חכמה	WISDOM	Sphere of the Zodiac (represented by Neptune)	The 4 Twos— Knights	Musk
3	BINAH	בינה	UNDER-STANDING	Sphere of Saturn	The 4 Threes— Queens	Myrrh, Civet
4	CHESED	חסד	MERCY	Sphere of Jupiter	The 4 Fours	Cedar
5	GEVURAH	גבורה	STRENGTH	Sphere of Mars	The 4 Fives	Tobacco
6	TIPHARETH	תפארת	BEAUTY	Sphere of Sol	The 4 Sixes— Princes	Olibanum
7	NETZACH	נצח	VICTORY	Sphere of Venus	The 4 Sevens	Benzoin, Rose, Red Sandal
8	HOD	הוד	SPLENDOR	Sphere of Mercury	The 4 Eights	Storax
9	YESOD	יסוד	FOUNDA-TION	Sphere of Luna	The 4 Nines	Jasmine, Ginseng, all Odoriferous Roots
10	MALKUTH	מלכות	KINGDOM	Sphere of the Elements (The Earth)	The 4 Tens— Princesses	Dittany of Crete

XLI	XL	XXXIV, XXXV, XIX	XXXVIII	XXXIX	XVI	XLV
Weapon	Stone	Gods	Animals	Plants	Colors	Magical Power
Swastika or Fylfat Cross, Crown [Lamp]	Diamond	Jupiter (Roman), Zeus (Greek), Ptah (Egyptian)	God	Almond in Flower	White brilliance	Union with God
Linga, the Inner Robe of Glory [Word, Hollow Tube]	Star Ruby, Turquoise	Janus (Roman), Athena (Greek), Amoun (Egyptian)	Man	Amaranth	Gray	The Vision of God
Yoni, the Outer Robe of Concealment. [Cup]	Star Sapphire, Pearl	Juno (Roman), Demeter (Greek), Maut (Egyptian)	Woman	Cypress, Opium Poppy	Black	The Vision of Sorrow
The Wand, Sceptre, or Crook.	Amethyst, Sapphire	Jupiter (Roman), Poseidon (Greek), Amoun (Egyptian)	Unicorn	Olive, Shamrock	Blue	The Vision of Love
The Sword, Spear, Scourge or Chain	Ruby	Mars (Roman), Ares (Greek), Horus (Egyptian)	Basilisk	Oak, Nux Vomica, Nettle	Scarlet Red	The Vision of Power
The Lamen or Rosy Cross.	Topaz, Yellow Diamond	Apollo (Roman), Apollo (Greek), Ra (Egyptian)	Phoenix, Lion, Child	Acacia, Bay, Laurel, Vine	Yellow	The Vision of the Harmony of Things (also the Mysteries of the Crucifixion)
The Lamp and Girdle	Emerald	Venus (Roman), Aphrodite (Greek), Hathoor (Egyptian)	Iynx	Rose	Emerald	The Vision of Beauty Triumphant
The Names and Versicles, the Apron	Opal, especially Fire Opal	Mercury (Roman), Hermes (Greek), Anubis (Egyptian)	Hermaphrodite, Jackal	Moly, Anhalonium Lewinii	Orange	The Vision of Splendor [Ezekiel]
The Perfumes and Sandals. [Altar]	Quartz	Diana (Roman), Diana of Ephesus (Greek), Shu (Egyptian)	Elephant	[Banyan], Mandrake, Damiana	Violet	The Vision of the Machinery of the Universe
The Magical Circle and Triangle	Rock Crystal	Ceres (Roman), Persephone (Greek), Seb (Egyptian)	Sphinx	Willow, Lily, Ivy	Citrine, olive, russet, and black	The Vision of the Holy Guardian Angel or of Adonai

Sephiroth	Food					
1						
2						
3						
4						
5						
6						
7						
8						
9						
10						

References

BIBLIOGRAPHY

Ariel, David. *The Mystic Quest.* New York: Schocken Books, 1988.

Buber, Martin (1878–1965). *Ten Rungs: Collected Hasidic Sayings.* New York: Citadel Press Book, 1995. First published 1947 by Schocken Books.

——————. *The Legend of the Baal-Shem.* Berkley: Audio Literature, 1992.

Crowley, Aleister. *The Book of the Law.* Boston: Red Wheel/Weiser, Centennial Edition, 2004.

——————. *The Book of Thoth.* York Beach, ME: Samuel Weiser, 1974.

——————. *The Goetia, The Lesser Key of Solomon the King.* San Francisco: Red Wheel, 2011.

——————. *Konx Om Pax.*

——————. *Magick in Theory and Practice.*

——————. *Magick, Liber ABA Book IV.* York Beach, ME: Weiser Books, 1998.

Dan, Joseph, et al. *The Early Kabbalah.* Mahwah, NJ: Paulist Press, 1986.

——————. *The Teachings of Hasidism.* West Orange, NJ: Behrman House, 1983.

DuQuette, Lon Milo. *Angels, Demons and Gods of the New Millenium.* York Beach, ME: Weiser Books, 1997.

——————. *The Chicken Qabalah of Rabbi Lamed Ben Clifford.* York Beach, ME: Weiser Books, 2001.

——————. *Understanding Aleister Crowley's Thoth Tarot.* York Beach, ME: Weiser Books, 2003.

Epstein, Perle. *Kabbalah: The Way of the Jewish Mystic.* Boston/London: Shambhala, 1988.

Fine, Lawrence, et al. *Safed Spirituality.* Mahwah, NJ: Paulist Press, 1984.

Fishbane, Michael. *Judaism*. San Francisco: Harper & Row, 1987.

Franck, Adolphe (1809–1893). *The Kabbalah (La Kabbale: ou la philosophie religieuse des Hebreux.* (Paris, 1843.) New York: Bell Publishing Co., 1915.

Gaon, Saadia. *The Book of Beliefs and Opinions (Kitab al-'Amanat wal-I'tikadat).* New Haven/London: Yale University Press, 1976.

Gikatilla, Joseph (1238–1323). *Gates of Light (Sha'are Orah).* San Francisco: HarperCollins, 1994.*

Hall, Manly. *Secret Teachings of All Ages.* Los Angeles: Philosophical Research Society, 1988.

Idel, Moshe. *Hasidism: Between Ecstasy and Magic.* New York: State University of New York, 1995.

——————. *Kabbalah: New Perspectives.* New Haven/London: Yale University Press, 1988.

——————. *Language, Torah and Hermeneutics in Abraham Abulafia.* New York: State University of New York, 1989.

——————. *The Mystical Experience in Abraham Abulafia.* New York: State University of New York, 1988.

——————. *Studies in Ecstatic Kabbalah.* New York: State University of New York, 1988.

Kaplan, Aryeh. *The Sefer Yetzirah.* York Beach, ME: Samuel Weiser, 1993.*

——————. *Meditation and Kabbalah.* York Beach, ME: Samuel Weiser, 1982.*

——————. *The Bahir (Sefer ha-Bahir,* 1176). York Beach, ME: Samuel Weiser, 1979.

Kircher, Athanasius. *Oedipus Aegyptiacus.* Rome: 1653.

Kraft, Anita. "How the Zohar Conceptualizes God." Unpublished manuscript, last modified 1994.

——————. "The Shekhinah." Unpublished manuscript, last modified 1994.

Levi, Eliphas. *Transendental Magic,* translated by A. E. Waite. York Beach, ME: Weiser Books, 1968.

---

* indicates additional suggested reading.

Mathers, S. Liddell MacGregor. *The Kabbalah Unveiled.* York Beach, ME: Samuel Weiser, 1968.

——————. *The Key of Solomon the King.* York Beach, ME: Weiser Books, 2000.

Meltzer, David. *The Path of Names.* Writings by Abraham Ben Samuel Abulafia (*Sha'erei Zedek, Gates of Justice*), and Joesph Gikatilla (*Sefer ha-Ot, The Book of Letters*). Berkley: Trigram Tree, 1976.

Mendes-Flohr, Paul. *Gershom Scholem: The Man and His Work.* New York: State University of New York, 1994.

Patai, Raphael. *The Jewish Alchemists.* Princeton, NJ: Princeton University Press, 1994.

Reuchlin, Johann (1455–1522). *On the Art of the Kabbalah* (*De Arte Cabalistica,* 1517). Introduction by Moshe Idel. Lincoln, NE: University of Nebraska Press, 1983.

Scholem, Gershom. *Major Trends in Jewish Mysticism.* New York: Schocken Books, 1974. First printed in 1946 by Schocken Books.*

——————. *The Messianic Idea in Judaism.* New York: Schocken Books, 1971.

——————. *On the Kabbalah and Its Symbolism.* New York: Schocken Books, 1965.*

——————. *On the Mystical Shape of the Godhead: Basic Concepts in the Kabbalah.* New York: Schocken Books, 1991. First printed Zurich: Rhein-Verlag AG, 1962.

——————. *Origins of the Kabbalah.* Princeton, NJ: Jewish Publication Society, Princeton University Press, 1987. First published in 1962 by Walter de Gruyter & Co.*

——————. *Sabbatai Sevi: The Mystical Messiah.* Princeton, NJ: Princeton University Press, 1973.

Seltzer, Robert. *Jewish People, Jewish Thought.* New York: Macmillan, 1980.

Sharf, Andrew. *The Universe of Shabbetai Donnolo* (ca. 913). Warminister: Aris & Phillips, 1976.

Verman, Mark. *The Books of Contemplation* (*Sefer ha-'Iyyun,* 1230). New York: State University of New York, 1992.

SEFER YETZIRAH TRANSLATIONS

Kalisch, Isidor. New York: L. H. Frank & Co., 1950.
Kaplan, Aryeh. York Beach, ME: Samuel Weiser, 1993.
Postel, William. 1552.
Westcott, William. London: 1893; rpt San Diego: Wizards Bookshelf, 1990.

SEFER HA-ZOHAR EXCERPTS 1275–1286

Berg, Philip. Dr. *The Zohar: Parashat Pinhas.* Jerusalem/New York: The Research Center for Kabbalah, 1988.
Matt, Daniel, et al. *Zohar: The Book of Enlightenment.* Ramsey, NJ: Paulist Press, 1983.
Scholem, Gershom. *Zohar: The Book of Splendor.* New York: Schocken Books, 1977. First published in 1949 by Schocken Books.
Tishby, Isaiah. *The Wisdom of the Zohar.* London/Washington: The Littman Library of Jewish Civilization, 1994.

MANUSCRIPTS AND PRIMARY TEXTS

GiNaT Egoz (Gikatilla)

Harba de Moshe (Merkevah)

Havdalah (Merkevah)

Haye Olam ha-Ba (Abulafia)

Hekhalot (Zohar)

Hekhalot Rabbati (Merkevah)

Hekhalot Zutreti (Merkevah)

Idra di-be-Mashkana (Zohar)

Idra Rabba (Zohar)

Idra Zutta (Zohar)

Kav ha-Middah (Zohar)

Ketavim Hadashim (Vital)

Mathnithin (Zohar)

Ma'aseh Bereshith (Merkevah)

Ma'aseh Merkevah (Merkevah)

Ma'ayan ha-Hokmah ('Iyyun Circle)

Merkevah Rabbah (Merkevah)

Midrash ha-Neelam (Zohar)

Otzar Eden ha-Ganuz (Abulafia)

Pardes Rimmonim

Rav Methivtha (Zohar)

Raya Mehemna (Zohar)

Raza de-Razin (Zohar)

Reuyot Yehezke (Merkevah)

Sava (Zohar)

Sefer ha-Bahir

Sefer ha-Emunah (Nachmanides)

Sefer ha-Hayyim (Provence)

Sefer ha-'Iyyun ('Iyyun Circle)

Sefer ha-Malbush (Merkevah)

Sefer ha-Ot (Abulafia)

Sefer ha-Razim (Merkevah)

Sefer Hasidim (Ashkenazie Hasidim)

Sefer Hekhalot (Merkevah)

Sefer Razi'el (Merkevah)

Sefer Yetzirah (Merkevah)

Sha'ar Orah (Gikatilla)

Sha'erei Zedek (Gikatilla)

Sheloshah 'Asar Kohot ('Iyyun Circle)

Shimmushe Tehillim (Merkevah)

Shiur Quomah (Merkevah)

Shivhe ha-Ari

Sifra de-Tseniutha (Zohar)

Sithre Ahra

Sithre Othioth (Zohar)

Sithre Torah (Zohar)

Tikkune Zohar (Zohar)

Yenuka (Zohar)

Zohar to the Song of Songs (Zohar)

ABOUT THE AUTHOR

ANITA KRAFT is an accomplished Qabalist and magician with twenty years of research, study, and practice. While traveling all over the world, she has attended a number of universities and studied religions as well as Jewish mysticism. Anita is a Bishop in the Ecclesia Gnostica Catholica, and a twenty-year initiate of the Ordo Templi Orientis. Visit her online at *www.magickqabalah.com*.

TO OUR READERS

Weiser Books, an imprint of Red Wheel/Weiser, publishes books across the entire spectrum of occult, esoteric, speculative, and New Age subjects. Our mission is to publish quality books that will make a difference in people's lives without advocating any one particular path or field of study. We value the integrity, originality, and depth of knowledge of our authors.

Our readers are our most important resource, and we appreciate your input, suggestions, and ideas about what you would like to see published.

Visit our website at *www.redwheelweiser.com* to learn about our upcoming books and free downloads, and be sure to go to *www.redwheelweiser.com/ newsletter* to sign up for newsletters and exclusive offers.

You can also contact us at *info@rrwwbooks.com* or at

Red Wheel/Weiser, LLC
665 Third Street, Suite 400
San Francisco, CA 94107